surprised by the Healer

Embracing Hope for Your Broken Story

linda dillow
dr. juli slattery

MOODY PUBLISHERS

CHICAGO

Library of Congress Cataloging-in-Publication Data
Names: Dillow, Linda.
Title: Surprised by the healer : embracing hope for your broken story / Linda Dillow and Dr. Juli Slattery.
Description: Chicago : Moody Publishers, 2016. | Includes bibliographical references.
Identifiers: LCCN 2015039126 | ISBN 9780802413406
Subjects: LCSH: Sexual abuse victims—Religious life. | Abused women—Religious life. | Christian women—Religious life. | Sex—Religious aspects—Christianity.
Classification: LCC BV4596.A2 D55 2016 | DDC 261.8/3272—dc23 LC record available at http://lccn.loc.gov/2015039126

We hope you enjoy this book from Moody Publishers. Our goal is to provide high-quality, thought-provoking books and products that connect truth to your real needs and challenges. For more information on other books and products written and produced from a biblical perspective, go to www.moodypublishers.com or write to:

Moody Publishers
820 N. LaSalle Boulevard
Chicago, IL 60610

3 5 7 9 10 8 6 4 2

To the nine brave women who shared their stories,
exalting the Healer and giving hope
to countless others with broken stories.

CONTENTS

Dear Friend,

*W*e are so grateful that you are holding *Surprised by the Healer* in your hands! Why? Because we believe this book will breathe hope into you—body, soul, and spirit. We began talking and praying about this book three years ago, long before we began to write it.

Over the course of decades, we have met many women who are suffering from wounds in the most intimate area of their lives—wounds caused by broken vows, past mistakes, sexual addictions, and the trauma of sexual abuse. Because this brokenness is so private, women typically don't reach out for hope or help. Instead, they limp along, assuming that their stories will never be rewritten.

Regardless of how put together they look, many of the women around you also have broken stories. This book is for you and for them. It contains the powerful stories of nine honest, brave women whose lives demonstrate that God is the healer of emotional, relational, and sexual brokenness. We pray that you will see that He has the power to redeem your pain and story too!

Whether you are single or married, young or not so young, no matter the circumstances of your brokenness, we invite you to be surprised by the Healer's work in your story.

May God be with you as you read,

Linda and Juli

1

Surprised by the Healer

*O*ur eyes scanned the delectable delights before us: pecan-crusted salmon, warm homemade rolls, and Mississippi mud brownies. No one would be dieting at this luncheon.

Twelve women encircled the table, talking as only women can about the enticing lunch that they didn't have to cook. No preparation, no cleanup—the meal was a cherished treat. But this special luncheon wasn't only about food but also an occasion to thank each woman for her work in bringing the Authentic Intimacy conference to Ohio.

As different women talked about their excitement for the conference, Ann's words caught our attention: "I want wives to see that it is a privilege to minister to their husbands sexually."

Perhaps you have an immediate idea of what kind of woman would make such a statement. Maybe you picture Ann as someone who lives in a fairy-tale land where everything looks picture perfect. Or maybe you assume she must have grown up in a nurturing and healthy home. In either case, you would be wrong. Ann's background is one of horrific sexual abuse and humiliation followed by promiscuity. She and her husband have struggled through three decades of healing, taking steps to learn to love each other emotionally, spiritually, and sexually.

Yet, here she was, advocating for God's beautiful design for sex in marriage. Are you surprised? We certainly were.

We are continuously (sometimes daily) amazed by the stories and testimonies we hear about Jehovah Rapha, the Healer. God is always surprising us with His creativity, power, and grace when it comes to healing. We want you to be surprised too, not just by the healing He has done in the women whose stories you will soon read but also by the healing He brings into the most intimate aspect of your life.

Between the two of us, we have ministered to women in the arena of sexual issues for several decades. Yes, we have some training on how to address brokenness using the tools of counseling and psychology. However, we have witnessed that the deepest healing only occurs through the presence of the Healer. Sexual brokenness is the deepest form of brokenness, and as such it requires the greatest depths of healing and restoration.

Every Woman's Pain

Rarely do we meet a woman who has not been, in some manner, scarred or wounded in the area of sexuality. At our Authentic Intimacy events, after a few hours of teaching on God's perspective of sex, we take live questions from the audience via text message. Visualize for a moment, a room packed with women. Young and old, single and married, from all walks of life. They have just heard that God cares about their sexual questions, secrets, and pain. They are now free to ask any question they want, anonymously. Can you imagine what questions come in? In a group of fifteen hundred women, we may get six hundred questions. They come pouring in, full of pain and desperation. Often, the women look "put together" and have grown up in church, but underneath is a rushing current of confusion and pain that they have never been given permission to reveal. Here are some of the questions women asked at our last event:

How can I enjoy my husband fully [sexually] when pornography and infidelity have come in and stolen so much from our marriage?

Does God hate me when I have sex with my boyfriend? Is He totally disconnected from me?

I started having sex at age fifteen. I had multiple sex partners and was sexually an adventurist until I was twenty-nine. My pseudo Christian husband exposed me to porn and S&M. He divorced me. Now what do I do with all the thoughts and shame I feel? God help me!

My pain is DEEP because my husband hasn't had sex with me in seven YEARS. What do I do with that pain? I recently overcame a year's long porn habit, and I don't want to ever go back there. But the pain of rejection runs deep.

I've been through molestation, parental abuse, promiscuity, rape, and infidelity. In marriage I never say no to sex with my husband, but I feel like I just want to please him, but inside I'm junk. But no one knows this about me.

I have a long past of sexual sin. I know I'm forgiven, but I can't let go of some of the memories. Sometimes a word, a song, or a smell bring them up again. Is there anything I can do to erase them from my memory?

As we read and respond to questions like these, we are often struck by the level of pain that can exist in a room of women. We look at the faces in the audience, and see they are eager to hear our responses. Each leans in as if to say, "She's not the only one who needs to know the answer. I could have written that question."

Friend, it's time we tear down the veneer and acknowledge that sexual brokenness is everywhere around us and within us. Just think of the ways that sex is creating deep pain and spiritual bondage within our churches and communities. Pornography, prostitution, sexual addictions, gender confusion, rape, incest, adultery, sexual harassment . . . the list of how sex has been distorted and twisted seems endless. This wonderful gift from God has become a source of profound pain for countless men and women. We believe that this is not just a random cultural phenomenon but is evidence of a vicious spiritual battle.

Sexuality is a powerful force. It draws us into relationships, compels us to risk being vulnerable, and is a key component of our identities as men and women. Within marriage sexual intimacy is the most sacred experience two people can share. However, sexuality can also be a devastating force for harm. There is no betrayal like an intimate betrayal. No shame as deep as sexual shame. And no sin that seems to stick to us like sexual sin.

Let's be honest. We are losing the battle over sexuality. Not just the battle "out there" in the culture but the battle in our own hearts and in our own homes. Why have so few Christian women experienced the healing and redemption that Ann's life displays? Why are so many Christian marriages destroyed because of infidelity, and so many of God's children walking with a dark cloud of sexual shame?

Tragically, many, many Christians believe that we are doomed to lose the battle of sexuality. They reason that some wounds are too deep, some people just too broken. After all, why would God care about sex? They may never say it, but the vast majority believe this lie: *When you give your life to Christ, He is able to redeem and clean up a lot of areas. However, there is one area that is beyond His redemptive healing power—your sexuality. You may be forgiven, but you can never be whole.*

We want to declare that this is a bold-face lie from the enemy. There is nothing too broken for God to heal.

Can God Really Heal Sexual Wounds?

Some of you, like many of the women we meet, are having a hard time believing this to be true. Perhaps you have bought into the lie that some wounds (particularly invisible sexual wounds) can never be healed. You believe that Jesus walked the earth and performed miracles and that He occasionally grants a miracle today; you also believe that God doesn't care about sex or that your sexuality is damaged beyond repair. So you put on a pretty face and limp through life with your deepest wounds compartmentalized so that the shame and pain don't bleed into the "real you."

We've got news for you. God offers more than life in silos. He wants to bring the power of His Word and His Spirit, making you a new creation in *all* areas of your being, including your sexuality. He desires to restore and redeem your sexual brokenness. Why? Because sexuality represents a powerful piece of the gospel. There is no greater picture of God's love than the covenant of marriage and the sacredness of sexuality.[1] When you invite God to heal your sexual brokenness, you're partnering with Him to restore His holy picture.

Our Lord God Almighty has many names, each declaring WHO He is. His name Jehovah Rapha boldly declares He is the Lord, our Healer. While at times we may need physical healing, our greater need is for spiritual healing. The most common use of *Rapha* in the Old Testament refers to spiritual healing.

Rapha means quite literally "to heal, make healthy."[2] *Rapha* is used more than sixty times in the Old Testament in reference to physical, emotional, or spiritual healing. Here are a few examples:

- In Genesis 20:17 God physically heals (*rapha*) a man, his wife, and his slave girls so that they can have children.
- In 1 Kings 18:30 Elijah repairs (*rapha*) the altar of Jehovah, which had been torn down. Here *rapha* clearly conveys the idea of physically restoring something to its "normal" or useful state.
- In Psalm 147:3 the psalmist refers to God as the healer of emotions. The psalm shows the tenderness and compassion of Jehovah Rapha, who heals (*rapha*) the brokenhearted and binds up their wounds.
- In Psalm 41:4 David cries out to Jehovah Rapha for spiritual healing. He pleads, "Lord [Jehovah], be merciful to me. Heal (*rapha*) my soul, for I have sinned against you."

Our God heals! *Rapha* clearly conveys the idea of restoring something to its "normal" state. We long for you to grasp that the Healer heals and restores sexual wounds.

Jehovah Rapha heals the brokenhearted. He lovingly lifts up His broken women and tenderly applies the salve of His healing presence to wounds caused by sinful choices, unhealthy beliefs, betrayal, pornography, and abuse. No evil done to you is so great that God cannot redeem it! God is for you in this! He longs for you to believe that He comes to you personally as Jehovah Rapha.

What Does God Promise to Heal?

Are you afraid to hope? Maybe you've hoped for healing before, only to experience bitter disappointment. Perhaps you've even had people say hurtful things to you like, "You're not healed because you don't have enough faith." Before we go any further, we want to clarify what we believe God promises about healing.

In this book you will read stories from women who have experienced dramatic, supernatural healing. You will also read stories from women whose healing appears to be incomplete. They still carry scars and wounds from traumatic events or betrayal. Why the difference?

While God promises to redeem us, to work all things together for the good of those who love Him and are called by Him (Romans 8:28), His healing looks different from person to person. Each healing is unique to that individual. In some cases, God takes away the physical impact of illness or the emotional pain of a traumatic memory. In others, He gives His wisdom and the strength to endure.

At times God heals the "temporal" temporarily, but He heals the eternal eternally. Let's put it this way. When Jesus walked on the earth, He chose to heal some physical ailments, such as leprosy, blindness, and other disabilities. In rare cases, He even raised the dead. However, those physical miracles were temporary for the sake of displaying the healing and redemption that is eternal.

When Jesus heard that His friend Lazarus had died, He was filled with sadness. It hurt Him to see His friends Mary and Martha grieve their brother. Jesus said something strange to His disciples: "For your sake I am glad that I was not there [to heal Lazarus], so that you may believe" (John 11:15).

Jesus didn't just raise Lazarus from the dead simply so he could live a couple more decades. That healing was temporary; His friend's body eventually decayed; Lazarus died a physical death, just as all humans do. Jesus raised Lazarus to impact people for eternity: that they might believe.

When Jesus healed, He did so for the purpose of pointing us to the eternal truth that He is the Son of God, able to forgive sin and set us free from spiritual bondage. In other words, God doesn't heal a woman of the pain of sexual abuse simply so that she can enjoy sex (although this is a wonderful gift!). His ultimate purpose in her healing, whether she is single or married, is that she will know that He is Lord, that He is her Healer, and that He has the power to redeem our lives from the pit.

In Matthew 9:1–8 we read about a man who was paralyzed. Everyone assumed the man has asked his friends to bring him to Jesus for physical healing. Jesus' surprising response reveals the man's deeper wound: "Take heart, son; your sins are forgiven." When onlookers doubted that Jesus could forgive sins, He said, "I want you to know that the Son of Man has authority on earth to forgive sins." Then Jesus turned to the paralyzed man and healed him physically. Note that Jesus first healed the man's spiritual wound, which was hidden, and then He healed his physical condition.

God has not promised to heal our temporary brokenness, although He can and sometimes does. What He does promise is to redeem completely those things that are everlasting: our hearts, souls, and spirits. Isaiah beautifully summarized our Healer's intention with these prophetic words about the Redeemer:

The Spirit of the Sovereign Lord is on me, because the Lord has anointed me to proclaim good news to the poor. He has sent me to bind up the brokenhearted, to proclaim freedom for the captives, and release from darkness for the prisoners, to proclaim the year of the Lord's favor and the day of vengeance of our God, to comfort all who mourn, and to provide for those who grieve in Zion—to bestow on them a crown of beauty instead of ashes, the oil of joy instead of mourning, and a garment of praise instead of a spirit of despair. They will be called oaks of righteousness, a planting of the Lord for the display of His splendor. (61:1–3)

Jesus quoted this passage early in His ministry (see Luke 4:18), declaring that He is the fulfillment of this prophecy. Oh yes, He made the blind see and the lame walk. But greater still were His unseen miracles.

When Jesus forgives our sins, He also heals our soul wounds, which are intricately intertwined with guilt and shame. No one can see this healing physically but they can see a changed life, a different outlook, a different demeanor. Precious friend, the Healer wants to meet you in this way!

Do you long for sexual healing? God's Word declares that there is healing for your deepest pains and disappointments. There is victory over your addictions, your past hurts, your past failures. Physical and spiritual healing are available to you when you run to the strong tower of Jesus, your Jehovah Rapha. If you are stuck in your sexual brokenness, run to Jehovah Rapha, the God Who Heals!

In these pages, you will meet nine courageous women who

have agreed to tell you their stories, to share with you how they moved from no hope and brokenness to hope and healing. They will tell you how the Healer invited them on a unique journey to redemption in the midst of brokenness. Some of their stories will amaze you. Some will bring you to tears.

When you meet Marian, you may be shocked that a pastor's wife has such a sordid past. But keep reading.

When you meet Ann, you may cringe, wondering, *How did she live through that horror? How can it be possible that she enjoys sex today?* But keep reading.

When you meet Amy, you may think, *No way! This kind of healing isn't possible. Does she live in a La La Land?* But keep reading.

Surprised by the Healer is not just about these women and how they came to know God as Jehovah Rapha, the God who heals. It is a personal invitation for you to know His healing too. Together the chorus of these nine testimonies extends to you this invitation:

Please, please don't stay in your brokenness. Jehovah Rapha invites you to heal. He is waiting to surprise you.

Are you ready to be surprised?

2

Marian's Story

Exchanging Lies for Truth

I gave my husband a most unexpected wedding gift: my cold shoulder.

For the first seven years of marriage—or 2,558 nights including leap year—I had no desire to learn the language of physical intimacy. My sexual shutdown shocked me, because I'd been sexually active for many years prior to meeting Nathan, my husband. While I had good reason to think something was wrong, instead of trying to get help and healing, I transformed our bedroom into a battlefield. Every evening I found something to argue about and fueled the fire until our communication shut down and I went to bed—alone.

When I look back, I can see that I was terrified of the vulnerability required for sexual intimacy. Even more I feared the flood of faces waiting for me in the surrender of our bedroom. Fighting was a sure way to ward off intimacy, and so I fought. Fiercely. Relentlessly. Mercilessly.

In those rare moments when love won and I ate my words of dissension, in those moments when I offered my best attempt at intimacy, memories would resurface. Things I'd forgotten would become clear again. Faces and names, words and smells, feelings of shame and rejection would overwhelm me. Memories of past sexual encounters paralyzed me. I longed to be safe in my marriage, but I was shackled by guilt over past sins with men long gone. I found that I could keep my arsenal of shame locked away as long as I didn't engage in sex with my husband. Consequently, I wanted to be left alone in love.

Except for the nights I didn't. Some nights I'd wait until Nathan's breathing had evened and then I'd roll over toward him. I wanted so badly to reach my hand out and just touch his back, knowing my one touch would speak my longing for healing.

But I never reached out. Not once for seven years. Instead, I numbered Nathan's breaths, counting the many ways I was failing. And I imagined what freedom must feel like. Freedom to invite my husband to find comfort in my physical affection. Freedom to love without shame. I imagined what it would feel like to be lost and entangled in my husband's love. I imagined healing.

Calling It What It Is

To say that I had sex outside of marriage before I met and married Nathan doesn't accurately describe my actions. I was promiscuous. You might ask, "What's the difference?" Sex outside of marriage can happen only once or twice. It can happen with a fiancé. It can happen with a boyfriend of six years. But promiscuity is a lifestyle of indiscriminate sex. It's sex without relationship, and sometimes it's relationships based on sex. It's engaging in casual sex with many different partners. In short, promiscuity is sexual chaos. This chaos was my reality for years.

Because the church is largely silent about the long-term impact of promiscuity, I was left alone with my shame and confusion, playing the part of a happy wife. In the silence, I started to wonder if my brokenness was beyond healing. I secretly feared that I disgusted God, just as I disgusted myself. I carried my brokenness as a prison sentence.

I was lonely, but I got used to it. I didn't even register pain most days.

An Invitation to Heal

It was in this dark place that the Healer met me. Ironically, it was when I hit rock bottom, the year we almost lost our marriage.

I had returned to seeking attention from men other than my husband and, in response, Nathan had clamped down. The tighter he held on to me, the more I rebelled. In that rebellion I started writing.

I decided to attend a writers conference, but Nathan did not want me to go. He was certain I would meet someone else. Uncompassionate toward his fears, I packed my suitcase anyway. My tires spewed gravel as I backed out of the driveway.

The first evening I found myself in an elevator with another writer. She asked me, "What's your book about?" so I pitched it. I hate small talk, but politely asked her the same question. She told me her novel was about a pastor whose marriage was falling apart even as he served to keep other marriages together. We exited the elevator and found chairs in the hallway so I could listen to the rest of the story God had given her to write, a story that sounded much like my real life.

A couple hours later, I headed back to my hotel room—mascara streaked, heart raw. The softening of my hardened heart had begun.

I opened the door to a beautiful bouquet of flowers, complete with a card: "I'm sorry. I hope God meets you this weekend. Love, Nathan." I plopped down onto my bed, put the card inside my Bible, and flipped open to the verses the elevator-author had shared with me.

Said the Lord to his rebellious people, Israel:

Why do you want more beatings?
Why do you keep on rebelling?
The whole head is hurt, and the whole heart is sick.
From the sole of the foot even to the head,
No spot is uninjured—wounds, welts, and festering sores
Not cleansed, bandaged, or soothed with oil . . .
(Isaiah 1:5–6 HCSB)

God called me out and named my problem: rebellion. As I realized this, I prayed, *I want healing, Lord! Reopen these old wounds if You have to. I can handle it. Do what You need to. I'm so tired of feeling damaged. It's been years and I'm still bruised and I desperately need You to heal me.*

And with that prayer, God began to work.

Seven years earlier, Jesus found me in a life of promiscuity, and I thought I could leave my messy past behind me. After all, I was a new creation! I mistakenly believed my salvation and my healing were synonymous. But they weren't. Seven years earlier, Jesus had asked to be my Savior. In that hotel room, He asked to be my Healer.

I accepted.

Visiting My Past

The Healer began my healing by taking me to the place I didn't want to go—my painful past. In the archaeological dig of my sexual history, God began to show me the lies that had been planted and embedded in my thinking.

I don't know why, but from a young age I was an attention-seeker. My validity and self-worth were rooted in how men responded to me. I saw myself as they saw me, and it wasn't pretty. With each breakup or one-night stand, I'd file away a lesson—a new deep-seated, intimacy-stealing lie—about who I was.

I was fifteen when my older boyfriend ignored me when I told him no. I looked at the clock when he started, and then again when he finished. Six minutes to womanhood. All the while I could hear cheers coming from the other side of the closed door.

Afterward, he took me out to fast food so we could talk.

"If you get pregnant or something, I'll pay to have it taken care of."

"What?"

"I'll pay for an abortion."

I hadn't thought of that. "Oh."

We ate a little more in silence.

"And there's one more thing."

I looked up at him, trying to sift through everything that had happened, trying to redefine our relationship now that we'd had sex.

"I don't think we're working out," he said between bites.

My entire teenage world came crashing down through the smell of garlic bread sticks and ready-made ravioli.

Within the month, he was dating someone else. They went to church together. I heard she had told him no, and he had listened.

The lies I embraced:

I am disposable.

My nakedness might be repulsive.

The next guy I dated never talked unless he was drinking. As soon as he was drunk, he was all hands and demands. Still, he didn't leave me after the first night we had sex. During our year of dating, I learned the lie that *substances create a numbness that should be part of the sexual experience.*

My last two years of high school, I dated a boy who worked in a video store that had a huge stash of adult videos. Several of the teachers from my high school—some married—would come in after work, darting through the aisles toward the private back room. Their choice to view pornography offered me an education outside the classroom, and taught me another lie: *If I want to keep a man's attention, I must perform well enough that pornography isn't needed.*

My boyfriend and I partied together, but my curfew was always earlier than his. On Monday mornings, I heard rumors about the girls he'd hooked up with after he dropped me off.

The lies I filed away included:

I am not enough and there's always someone else willing to fill the gap.

Performance, performance, performance will secure love.

When we broke up, I started waiting tables. Restaurants were a magical place. Food, fun, and recreational drugs everywhere. I managed to take a full scholarship and dispose of it in less than a semester as I entangled myself in the world of cocaine, prescription pills, Ecstasy, and anything else I was foolish enough to put in my arm, up my nose, or in my lungs. Because I dated guys who sold these drugs, I never had to pay cash for them, and I embraced the lie that *sex is a commodity. Trade it wisely.*

These lies guided my choices and banished the prospect of intimacy.

At twenty-one, I became a believer in Christ. At twenty-two, I met and married Nathan, a pastor, no less.

Despite my newfound faith and Nathan's love, my attitude toward sex was hardened. I believed I was just a product; I could be discarded, traded for someone more desirable, or consumed and left empty.

As God revealed the lies that I had believed, I began to question Him. Where was He in those years? Where was He when I was lonely? Why didn't He find me sooner? Why didn't He stop me? Why was I allowed to profane that which was sacred—sex? Why was intimacy so foreign to me?

God didn't respond to my accusations. Instead, He filled me with comfort and peace—with His Holy Spirit. That night in my hotel room the Healer taught me my first lesson in intimacy: *Presence is more powerful than a thousand words of explanation.*

Awakening a Desire to Draw Closer

When I arrived home from that writers conference and carried my suitcase into our bedroom, I stood in the doorway of our battlefield. For the first time, I began to hope that the words above our bed, a quote from the Song of Solomon, could someday be true: "This is my beloved; this is my friend."

My rebellion—my hardness of heart—was over, seven years after I'd come to trust Jesus. Finally, I was coming to know Him.

Now that I had stopped fighting my husband, I wanted to draw closer to him. The first step was to talk with Nathan. The conversation went like this:

"Honey, I think I'm tired of sex."

He said nothing, so I continued. "There has to be something more," I announced, "something we're missing."

"We can try again tonight and see," he offered sacrificially.

"No, no, no. You're not hearing me. I mean there has to be more to sexual intimacy than just sex."

It had to be true. I could feel it.

Being a rational gal, I decided I needed an accurate definition of sex. I wanted to go to trusted sources that could not be argued against, like the dictionary. I also wanted to go to Scripture. If a theology of intimacy existed, I determined to uncover it.

I went to *Webster's* first.

sex (n.) 1. the sphere of interpersonal behavior esp. between male and female most directly associated with, leading up to, substituting for, or resulting from genital union.

That definition didn't entice me—at all. No wonder I was tired of sex!

I tried another word via the good man, Webster.

intimate (adj.) 1. marked by a very close physical, mental, or social association, connection, or contact; fused, interwoven.

This definition captured what I longed for: the ability to fuse and weave myself with my husband on multiple levels—physical, mental, social, and, I would add, spiritual. I wanted to connect with my husband emotionally, intellectually, and spiritually for the purpose of finding physical intimacy too.

Insight dawned on me as I looked at the words again,

Heart.
Mind.
Soul.
Body.

Clarity came so strongly I could hardly breathe. These words were familiar to me. Was it possible that Scripture had a formula for intimacy with my husband? I flipped to Deuteronomy 6:4 and then cross-referenced to Matthew, floored by what I knew was waiting for me there. "Love the Lord your God with all your heart, mind, soul, and strength" (paraphrase of Matthew 22:37 and Dueteronomy 6:4). Heart. Mind. Body. Soul.

I suddenly realized that the path to physical and spiritual intimacy looked like this:

Heart + Mind + Body + Soul = All of me
Loving God with all of me = Spiritual intimacy

I began to see that what had been stolen from me so many years ago wasn't simply my purity but also a healthy sense of my personhood. My sexuality—my longings, desires, and identity—had been marred, and my brokenness was blocking me from giving all of myself to my husband, and, ultimately, to God. When I realized all this, I invited the Healer to replace the lies I had believed with His truth about sexuality so that I could experience His plan for intimacy with Nathan.

I had rejected sex in my marriage because it seemed like a cheap replacement for what I really desired—intimacy. I longed to know and to be known in every part of my being. I wanted this with my husband and I wanted this with God.

If intimacy was really about this deep connection, I had a huge roadblock. As a young woman, I had learned and believed that I was undesirable. I had a long list of reasons to back this up. I knew that parts of me would be repulsive to God and to my husband. But God was telling me that He wanted me to love Him with my whole self, not just the undamaged parts.

God desires me. I am desirable. That's a powerful realization.

Before I could experience true intimacy in my marriage, this truth had to sink into my heart and soul. If I knew that God accepted and loved my whole self, perhaps I could have the courage to be totally vulnerable with Nathan.

A New Beginning

I could trust God with my emotions, thoughts, body, and soul. But trusting another human required much deeper levels of vulnerability. As I became aware of the walls I had built to keep myself safe, I began naming and identifying the obstacles to intimacy that I had built.

Even in marriage, sex can be a transaction instead of an act of intimacy. One of the toughest barriers I had to overcome was the belief that I was a commodity. In my mind, the transaction went something like this: My husband uses me for his pleasure. In return, I engage with him sexually for security. Romantic, isn't it?

I had never asked Nathan about his views on sex. We just fought about it. I knew he wanted physical intimacy more than I was willing to give it, but I had no idea why he wanted it. It was time for me to sit down and have another conversation with him.

So I asked him, "Why do you want sex all the time?"

"Really? You have to ask that?"

"Yes. Although I'm guessing it's because you're a man and men want sex."

"Women want sex too," he said.

"Then maybe you should have married one of the women who want it all the time," I retorted. (Not exactly an intimacy-inviting response!)

"I want sex because it's when I feel closest to you."

"That's sort of gross. And obvious."

"No, it's not," he paused, making sure I was looking at him. "Really. I feel like we are the closest—the most intimate—like it's just you and me when we are making love. It's when I feel closest to you not just physically but emotionally. And I feel like I have your full attention, which is nice."

"Oh."

I wanted to say the same thing in return, but I couldn't—not yet, anyway. Instead I embraced his statement as truth. It was his truth, and I planned on repeating it over and over in my mind until it was my truth too.

And that is exactly what I did.

When thoughts came that sex was dirty and degrading, or when Nathan asked me about being sexually intimate and I wanted to give some sassy retort, I reminded myself that we were closest to each other when we were making love.

When I was full of criticism and had a mental list of all the reasons Nathan didn't deserve sex that evening, I reminded myself that our sexual intimacy was an expression of our intellectual, emotional, and spiritual closeness. It was about us reaching toward each other with the deepest intent to connect.

When the lies came whispering that sex was all about his pleasure and his gain, I rewrote them with my husband's truth. Sex, for him, was his expressed desire to be close to me.

Healing, for me, was reminding myself over and over again about these truths. It was so simple and so hard. Over and over again I had to rewrite lies with truth. I had learned to view myself as an object. I used my body as a means of securing relationships and my appearance for gathering male attention. I had learned responsiveness, but not assertiveness, because I still viewed sex as a tool for pleasure rather than an invitation to intimacy. I needed to rewrite my understanding of sexuality and to rediscover the beauty of my own femininity. The transformation took months.

During this same time I was taking a class about the Wisdom Literature in the Old Testament. One of the books we studied was the Song of Solomon. The erotic poetry helped me to be able to look at all parts of the human body—mine and my husband's—and see artistry and perfection and beauty. Over time, sensuality became a vast and beautiful land I couldn't wait to rediscover.

When Failure Comes

Nathan and I were relishing the beauty of our healed intimacy when I became pregnant with our fifth child and we moved across country. I finished my degree, and around the same time we bought a house that needed a lot of work. Consequently, I was exhausted before our youngest even arrived. After she was born, I was grateful for the six weeks of medically induced sexual abstinence.

But something happened in those six weeks.

I shut down again. Completely.

Six weeks stretched into twelve weeks. Twelve weeks spanned five months. Our daughter was six months old, and we'd only had sex twice. Nathan was hurt, and I felt like a total failure.

I cried out to God. What had happened to my healing?

The Healer reminded me that I had practiced disconnecting for years. It would take time to make connection and intimacy my first language. I needed to embrace grace.

Today, Nathan and I are back to where I'd hoped we'd be, and our intimacy is somewhat sweeter for the failure. I learned I can put my mind in it, I can commit my heart to it, I can open my body in invitation, and I can fill my spirit with an overflow of God's love for my husband.

Healing and intimacy require hard work. While I can't hang them on the wall like a piece of art, I can still feel their tangible effects. I desire my husband and am free to love him with all of me—mind, body, soul, and heart. I am free to open my arms to him in invitation. I am free to be fully present and alive in the moment. Truly, this is freedom, for when I lie in the dark, I'm now filled with light.

You Are Invited . . . to Exchange Lies for Truth

In 1999, John F. Kennedy Jr., his wife, Carolyn, and Carolyn's sister Lauren died in a tragic plane crash off the coast of the Atlantic Ocean. The primary cause of the crash was that John was not "instrument rated" as a pilot. In other words, novice pilots navigate by what they see. Instrument-rated pilots have learned to fly by the instrument panel, even if the instruments seem to contradict what feels right when they look out the window.

The weather obscured his vision and perception, and John thought he was flying much higher than he was. The instruments in a plane are not deceived by clouds or fog like human judgment can be. They record altitude, air speed, and direction based on the unchanging laws of physics rather than perception. If John had trusted his instrument panel instead of what felt right, he may still be alive today.

Have you ever considered that you could be headed toward disaster for a similar reason? Every day, you make decisions about your choices and relationships based on what you believe about sexuality. Is what you believe based on an unchanging truth or based primarily on what "feels right"?

Many women live by "looking out of the window of the cockpit" of their lives. They make decisions about their sexuality by evaluating what they see and hear. Marian's story demonstrates this. Although she was a follower of Christ, her decisions about intimacy and sexuality were based on a skewed set of beliefs. Once Marian realized how lost she was in lies, she developed a voracious hunger to know God's perspective about her sexuality.

The unfailing instrument panel of a Christian's life is God's Word. Marian wanted to become an "instrument-rated" Christian who embraced God's wisdom about sexuality rather than living by familiar lies. James 1:6 tells us that a person who doubts God's wisdom is like someone driven and tossed around by the wind. The "winds" of our culture's views on sexuality have devastated far too many Christian women who were not rooted in God's truth.

Are you desperate to know God's wisdom about sex? His truth about you? Are you confused, as Marian was, about the relationship between sex and intimacy? Do you wonder why your sexuality has been shackled with shame rather than freedom? What you think about sex actually matters. If your thoughts on sex are based on lies, as Marian's were, your wrong thinking will eventually lead you to pain and difficulty.

Oh, how many Christian women have surrendered their lives to Jesus, except for this one little compartment called "sexuality"! While Jesus may be Lord, they reserve the right to define truth for themselves in the bedroom. This is where Marian found herself seven years into marriage. Her sexuality was still in bondage to the lies the enemy had written on her heart many years earlier. The Healer invited her to shine His truth upon her damaged soul as He whispered, "You will know the truth, and the truth will set you free" (John 8:32).

Exposing Lies

God says that when we accept Christ as our Savior, we become new creatures. Old things pass away and *all things* become new (2 Corinthians 5:17). Did you notice there is no exception clause in "all things" becoming new? All things include your sexuality.

The Bible actually has quite a bit to say about sex and sexuality. Yet many of us never consider that God's truth about sex can expose and set us free from the lies Satan has told us about sexuality. God's healing shouldn't stop at the threshold of your bedroom.

The battle for sexuality is rooted in how we think and what we believe about sex. As long as Marian's beliefs about sexuality were shackled by lies, sex in her marriage would be stilted and stifled. The same is true in each of our lives. Our sexuality may be demonstrated in our actions, but our actions are just an overflow of what we believe. Friend, the journey of healing is all about exchanging lies for truth.

Regardless of what our "everything goes" world says about sex, God created us as sexual beings for a purpose. He made a man's and woman's body to fit together. It was His design that sex should be so powerful, so pleasurable, and the means by which we have children.

Unfortunately, our enemy has his own designs on sex. His design is to distort. Satan is never creative, only destructive. He lies when he tells you that freedom comes through sleeping with whoever you want. He lies about God's goodness by telling you that preserving sex for marriage is restrictive and old fashioned. He lies when he tells you that your sexual past disqualifies you from God's grace. And he lies when he tells you that it's your body, your choice. "Do you not know that your bodies are temples of the Holy Spirit . . . Therefore honor God with your bodies" (1 Corinthians 6:19–20).

Marian accepted God's invitation to pursue the truth about her sexuality when she asked Him to begin exposing the lies that had been stored in her heart as a child and teenager. She had no idea how distorted her understanding of sexuality and intimacy was. But the Holy Spirit gently began exposing the lies that sabotaged intimacy in her marriage. One lie after the other . . .

> *I am disposable.*
> *My nakedness is repulsive.*
> *I must perform to compete with porn.*
> *I am not enough.*
> *My husband only wants my body.*
> *I'm an object.*
> *Sex is just a commodity.*

Marian told us, "The gracious Healer didn't reveal these lies without a purpose. Now I was desperate for God's truth."

Are you desperate for God's truth? Asking God to reveal the lies you believe about sex and your sexuality might feel like asking the dentist to do an unnecessary root canal. *I'm getting along just fine!* you might reason. *Why do I need to unearth painful things from my past?* If so, don't fool yourself. The untrue words that were planted in our hearts years ago have a hidden, unseen effect on our ability to give and receive love. Children chant, "Sticks and stones may break my bones but words will never hurt me," but Scripture says that words have the power of death and life (Proverbs 18:21). God does not reveal lies to bring us more pain but to allow His healing truth to shine in the dark places.

Embracing Truth

Marian was saturated in her pain when she discovered God didn't just make her a body but body, soul, and spirit. Her soul was numb to the deeper purpose of her sexuality. Every invitation for sex in her marriage felt more like an obligation than a celebration. She felt all she had to offer was an overused body. Sex had lost all meaning and had become only about two bodies groping for release.

The truth? Many women who are *sexually active* have no idea how to be *sexually intimate*. Sexual activity without intimacy soon becomes a sham, a cheap substitute for true connection.

God's love for Marian and Nathan was too great to allow them to stay stuck. God invited Marian to walk toward truth and ultimately freedom. She and Nathan began to experience that freedom in their marriage when lies were exposed and replaced by truth. The exchange went something like this:

The Enemy's Lie: Sex is all about performance.
God's Truth: Sex is about intimate presence.

The Enemy's Lie: Sex is a replacement for intimacy.
God's Truth: Sex is an expression of deep intimacy.

The Enemy's Lie: My body is an object to be used by my husband.
God's Truth: My husband's desire for me is an invitation to be known and loved.

The Enemy's Lie: My sexuality is completely separate from my devotion to God.
God's Truth: God cares about my sexuality, my healing, and sexual intimacy in my marriage.

God used His Word to teach Marian the truth about her sexuality. She discovered that love and intimacy are about sharing all of who you are—loving with your heart, your mind, your body, and your soul. Her "aha" moment was realizing that sex was meant to be a full expression of intimacy, not just bodies groping for a pleasurable release. This change in Marian's thinking translated into the transformation of her marriage.

As you look at the "horizon" of your relational and sexual life, does it seem chaotic and disorienting? Perhaps you can recognize lies that have misguided your choices for a long time. Here's some great news. The Bible is not some archaic, stuffy book. It contains words of truth that can set you free! When you choose to fix your eyes on God's truth, the Healer can transform your life, your marriage, and your approach to sexuality.

Bringing Truth Home

When God brings truth into our lives, He also gives us opportunities to act upon it. It's not enough for you to believe that sex is sacred. You must also make choices that reflect that truth. For Marian this meant walking these new truths into her bedroom.

For seven years she had a plaque with this beautiful verse hanging over her bed: "His mouth is full of sweetness. And he is wholly desirable. This is my beloved and this is my friend" (Song of Solomon 5:16 NASB). The words were more of a taunt than an inspiration until Marian began to pursue a relationship that reflected such intimacy.

We often say we believe the Bible, but our actions prove otherwise. We make real-life decisions based on our own "wisdom" and understanding. An instrument-rated pilot is one who actually makes life-and-death decisions based on the dials in front of him instead of trusting his instincts. Friend, what about you? Do your sexual choices demonstrate that you trust the instrument panel of God's truth or your own wisdom?

David experienced God's truth infiltrating and cleansing the most intimate area of his life, "Behold, You desire truth in the innermost being, and in the hidden part You will make me know wisdom" (Psalm 51:6 NASB). Marian experienced a radical transformation in her marriage because she was willing to place her trust in God's unchanging truth, allowing it to seep into the innermost being. Her testimony prompts an invitation, an invitation for you to pursue and embrace God's truth about your sexuality. It's our prayer that you accept the invitation and surrender this very personal area of your life to the truth and Lordship of Jesus Christ.[1]

1. Portions of this chapter are used by permission from the book by Marian Green *Inviting Intimacy: Overcoming the Lies of Shame,* releasing July, 2016 (Wesleyan Publishing House: wphstore.com).

3

Hope's Story

Coming Out of Hiding

A romantic novel with a few sex scenes. A sexual chat room, just for the sake of a little fun and excitement. Harmless, right?

Many women who are otherwise devoted to the Lord and their families indulge in what has come to be called "mommy porn." The fact that millions of women say they see nothing wrong with reading erotica or visiting adult chat rooms doesn't make these activities less dangerous or perverted. They may, in fact, tap into and reveal sexual brokenness that has been buried and ignored for years.

This was the case with me.

But by the sovereign grace of God, my path crossed with Juli Slattery's when I was asked to review a book Juli wrote with Dannah Gresh in response to *Fifty Shades of Grey*. The following blog post and ensuing messages between Juli and me will give you a glimpse of what the Healer has done and is currently doing to set me free! He didn't expose my sexual brokenness to condemn me but to invite me to come out of hiding so that I could be healed.

BLOG POST: APRIL 18

There comes a time when you have to do something that takes you OUT of your comfort zone. Something that you feel prompted by the Holy Spirit to change. And when the catalyst for that change lands in your path . . . or your email box . . . you have to recognize that NOW is the time to answer that call.

The time for me came when I was asked to review a book by Juli Slattery and Dannah Gresh called *Pulling Back the Shades.* My heart pounded. Would I? Would I be willing to share the very thing that I feel shame about? Would I be willing to bare my soul in order to help someone else heal?

I prayed. I pled. I begged. Everything in me wanted to say NO, but I made a promise to let GOD lead me this year. I made a promise to say YES to the things that will make my life beautiful. So I said YES.

The book arrived. It took me a WEEK to open it. A week! I had another week to read it. I couldn't do it. It made me feel scared. Ashamed. Completely undone. *It's just a book for heaven's sake!*

You see, this book addresses a secret that I have held close to my heart. A secret that I have hidden. The one thing that I won't even admit to myself . . . my husband . . . my psychiatrist . . . or my God. I so hate this thing about me that I avoid facing it at any cost. Now the book is looking me in the face and I hear HIM calling me . . . *READ. READ ME. Heal. Baby girl . . . there's healing here if you'll just let Me heal you.*

I weep. I run. I hide. The book is underneath my bed. I start reading. I can't read any more. I put it down. I'd much rather pretend my world is perfect. That there's not this big, huge, ugly sin-stained scar in my soul.

I finally admit after two weeks that I have to finish this book. So I read. And I start to cry . . . and yell . . . and fight. Fight against this secret that eats me alive. And when I'm done reading I know I have to admit WHY I've read the book.

I have to quit hiding from myself . . . from God. Right here. Right now.

I am the woman Dannah and Juli are speaking to in this book. Here is the short version of my story.

At seven I was sexually abused.

At eight I began masturbating.

At twelve I was introduced to pornography.

At twelve I began reading erotica.

The pornographic images haunted me. They reinforced the thoughts I had about myself: *I am a sinful, dirty child.*

When I was sad, stressed, or anxious, I used masturbation as a comfort mechanism. The Internet just made my struggle with pornography worse because it made access so easy and private. It was my little secret. The porn images led to fantasy images that were fueled by the books I was reading. Even though I was a child, I found it easy to check erotica out from the library. The erotic books led to erotic stories online and X-rated videos.

I've struggled with porn, erotica, and masturbation my entire life. Yes. Even after I got married. Even as I worked through the issues of abuse. Even as I prayed and cried and called myself a daughter of God. A mother. Pornography has haunted me since I was twelve years old. It's ugly. I hate it . . . and I just want it GONE.

With this book, Juli and Dannah have gently guided me to a place of safety where I can be real and honest. *I KNOW I'm not alone.* I know I can admit who I am and that my Creator will heal me . . . and save me . . . and take that horrible thing that happened to me as a child completely away. And I know now that I have to share this publically. Even if it costs me my friends . . . family . . . it will not cost me the love of my Savior.

APRIL 19

Dear Hope,

Someone recently sent me a link to the review of *Pulling Back the Shades* that you wrote on your blog. I'm praising the Lord for how He is working in your life! It took so much courage for you to write what you shared. I really admire you! Something was "broken" when you took that step of faith. You put a stake in the ground.

I know that God will guide you in your healing as you seek Him. We at Authentic Intimacy would love to be a part of that. Our Bible study, *Passion Pursuit*, is a powerful tool to help God's truth replace the "junk" regarding sexuality and will help you put into practice your desire to honor Him in this area of your marriage. It is a ten-week study, comprised of a fun workbook and accompanying DVD. If you would like to go through the study (alone or with a few friends), I would love to send you a copy as a gift and investment in the work God is doing in and through you.

I'd also love to hear more of your story as you feel comfortable sharing.

May the power of the resurrected Lord be within you. Blessings!

Juli

APRIL 19

Dear Juli,

God is answering my deepest cry! After you sent me the message on Facebook this morning, something compelled me to be a bit more courageous. My husband does not usually read my blog, which makes it seem safe to me. So I asked him if we could talk. He wanted to know about what and why. I finally just walked over to the bed and handed him *Pulling Back the Shades* and said, "Because of this."

What happened next I couldn't have orchestrated in a thousand years! I was able to tell him the thing I needed to . . . to be honest and vulnerable and open . . . to be real with the very person that I should be real with. Other than my stomach feeling like it was in my throat . . . and my heart beating out of my chest . . . it was healing . . . and incredible. And in this most vulnerable moment, I finally caught a glimpse of what wholeness is. And I wept . . . and I am still weepy . . . and overwhelmed.

So I absolutely know that God orchestrated my reading of this book . . . and your offering me help with the *Passion Pursuit* study. I would be fine with sharing my story . . . just not sure where to start. And I like to ramble. LOL. But very LONG story made short.

I am the product of a teen mother and a pedophile father, and a long family history of incest. The church twisted things to the point that I believed that sex was the origin of sin, and so I concluded that I WAS SIN.

Worst of all . . . during this time . . . I was also involved in incest (being molested and molesting) with my brothers and cousins. (Typing this out loud makes me feel so horrible . . . even still . . . after years in therapy.) So when I met my future husband at age seventeen, my opinion of myself was that I was dirty and not worthy of being loved. The funny thing is that HE was the only one who was respectful of me. Because of my fear, I didn't share much of my past with him. He didn't ask. I didn't tell.

When I became a mother, my past caught up with me to the point that I was suicidal. I started taking medication and entered therapy. It's been a long HARD journey. I thought I was doing okay, until the day I found out that my father molested other children and was going to jail for it. My entire life fell apart.

This process brought out so many things that I have kept hidden. The memories of the way my dad would make me feel, the uncomfortable hugs, the times he'd hold me and I wanted to scramble as fast as I could. The time he disappeared with my daughter at a family function and I FREAKED, and never could explain it.

I received a copy of the police report about him. In it he justifies what he did: "I did it to my own daughter, and . . . she's fine."

That statement broke something in me. BECAUSE I'M NOT FINE!

When *Pulling Back the Shades* showed up, I was at a crossroads. I felt horrible, like I was leading a double life. I was a homeschooling, Christian mom blogger—and I had developed a fantasy world where I would retreat whenever I faced emotions I couldn't handle. I'd imagine what it would be like to be in the type of relationship I wanted, and resented my husband for not being the person of my dreams. I couldn't see the good in our relationship, only the bad. *Pulling Back the Shades* helped me see where erotica and porn were taking me. The next step would be leaving my husband to act out my fantasies.

Now I feel hope that I can address the root of my issues and be whole. It's all intertwined: my past, my distorted views about sex and about myself. The thing is that I have FINALLY caught a glimpse of what sexual intimacy is supposed to be. That's what I want. And I want GOD.

I've long thought that what my abusers stole from me was my innocence. No. What they stole from me was my soul. And I want it BACK. I want to be completely whole. I want to feel love and to love. I want to know what it's like to have intimacy in a marriage, not just a "good sex life." I want to know what it's like to be completely comfortable with myself so that I no longer have to hide. I want to know what it's like to be connected to God, to my husband, to my life.

So, that's my story, It's been a journey. Even as I send this my stomach hurts. My heart feels the little girl in me that is scared. But my soul is screaming for joy because I know that healing is coming.

Blessings to you,

Hope

MAY 8

Dear Juli,

When you tell God you will allow Him to heal you, He does. But what I'm discovering is that the root of my problem was deep. So I read a book about my deepest shame, shared it publically, shared it with my husband, who in turn is vacillating between feelings of pain, love, and rejection.

We've NEVER had an issue with sex in our marriage. What's been missing is intimacy. My ability to let sex mean love. But I see now that we need that in our relationship. I need that. Even though we've had sex, we've never been "ONE" flesh. Never in twenty years. Yet I can see that coming. I feel like I'm dating my husband all over again. My choice to absolutely trust and surrender to another person——that was violated as a child. I'm terrified beyond belief, but I'm allowing my heart to be open.

Anyway, I just wanted to let you know and to THANK YOU for reaching out to me. You are a precious sister in the kingdom. God is using you to change many lives. Mine is one of them.

Have a blessed day,

Hope

MAY 9

Dear Hope,

Thank you for sharing your journey. I've been praying for you. I praise the Lord for how He is bringing healing into your marriage! Your steps have been ordained by Him. How beautiful to watch them unfold. I will keep praying as you continue to pursue Jesus and your husband with your WHOLE heart. There can be fear and pain when the Lord unfreezes a part of your heart that has been paralyzed. It's hard to explain, but to be alive usually means feeling not just new joys but also new pain and fear. He will give you strength and peace.

Blessings, my sister.

Juli

JUNE 19

Hi, Juli,

I've managed to get a little further on the *Passion Pursuit* Bible study. But I took a break. I've been struggling with the whole Song of Solomon being an erotic book in the Old Testament thing. I've been taught all my life that sex is sinful. I'm having trouble making the switch to believing that God actually says it's good. I'm still working on it.

I will say that something amazing has happened: I feel redeemed from the pull that the erotica had on me all these years. It's as if a heavy weight has gone. Speaking light into the darkness DID make a difference. And when I think of what happened to me as a little girl . . . the images . . . they're gone. *I can't retrieve them.* I know what happened. I remember that. But the images and the horrible dirty feeling? Gone! I'm still overwhelmed by it all.

So now I feel like I'm being remade. I'm watching the glorious thing the Father is unfolding. And I just smile. And let Him do what He's going to do.

Thank you again. For everything. For taking on a subject that the church has ignored or doesn't want to talk about.

For letting the Father use you to bring healing to the heart of the little girl I was and letting the woman I am arrive.

Blessings,

Hope

JULY 24

Hi, Juli,

Remember when you first emailed me, how I felt broken and wanted to feel love and to love back? I wrote that on April 19. I have to update, because I wanted to let you know that following the Father's lead has *helped a little girl become the woman she was meant to be!*

Last month my husband took our youngest on a short trip. I stayed home because I had to attend a homeschool conference. A couple of girlfriends came over, and we were chatting about how ridiculous our teens were with their selfies. So next thing you know, I sent my husband a selfie and a little note, telling him I'd have a surprise for him when he got home.

Okay. I didn't expect the impact my text would have—not on my husband but on ME. Flirting with him in a text, that playful suggestion, broke a wall. A wall that has been around my heart ever since I was a little girl. And that little break flooded my soul with love. I bared my heart and soul to this man I've been married to for almost twenty-one years like I never have. As I shared everything, and he listened, I realized that finally I was letting myself be completely vulnerable.

That little set of text exchanges has done something in our marriage. My husband has my heart. He's never had it before. It's all his. AND, I have his. AND I KNOW IT. I can feel it. Like we're connected. At the heart. And this is what it feels like to be in love. Oh, my soul . . . rejoice!

So we were able to have a night alone on Sunday. And I gave him the rest of me, and now I know why it says the two are one flesh. All these years I've missed the best part! It's not about biology or bodies or sex. It's love and a communion of souls.

I am still smiling at how this has changed our marriage. My husband sent me a message the other day, "What on earth happened to you?" I just smiled and said, "Jesus happened." He replied, "I can tell. You're different. I like it." Made my day! I feel like we just got married . . . so sappy!

Blessings & Hugs,

Hope

NOVEMBER 16

Hi, Juli,

I can't believe how God is healing our marriage right in front of my eyes. I realize that I was taught a lie my whole life. When I read *Pulling Back the Shades,* I realized my mind never grew up——it was damaged by erotica and pornography. *Passion Pursuit* has opened my eyes and I see Scripture differently. God is giving me back my purity.

So on our twenty-first wedding anniversary, I gave my husband a pure bride! It was beautiful and holy. My abuse does not define me. Wrong teaching about sex does not define me. God's Word defines me! I am new! I have become a totally transformed woman.

You Are Invited . . . to Come Out of Hiding

"Ollie, Ollie oxen free! Come out, come out wherever you are!" These are phrases we used as children in games of hide-and-seek. They mean that it's safe to come out of hiding. Do you wonder what life would be like if it were truly safe to come out of hiding?

Hide-and-seek isn't the only hiding game we first learned as children. Before we were even aware of it, we were taught subtly or overtly that some things should be kept secret. Mom and Dad's arguments, Uncle Jack's felony, and Dad's toupee. And then there are our own secrets. No one had to tell you to bury the shame of sexual abuse, your struggle with porn, masturbation, or cutting. You just intuitively knew that not all truth should be exposed.

As you read Hope's story, were you struck by her courage? When she decided to come out of hiding, she didn't do it halfway. Her desire to be free was so great that she risked everything in the pursuit of healing.

Hope's life on the outside appeared to be intact. She was a homeschooling mom, a blogger, a Christian, and a wife. But her secrets were killing her and strangling the potential for oneness in her marriage. There is power in keeping secrets, a power that works to keep us isolated in shame and helplessness.

What Keeps Us Captive to Our Secrets?

All of us know, to some extent, the stress and duplicity of hiding something. On the outside we appear to be a confident Christian who knows the right words to speak and how to act. But on the inside is a secret self who has thoughts and desires that we never want to admit. Sometimes we even have two different sets of friends; friends with whom we have to watch what we say and do in order to keep things about ourselves hidden, and friends with whom we don't because they won't challenge us in our sin.

We can only keep up the tension and stress of hiding for so long. Deep within us is a cry for authenticity and consistency. So what keeps us so bound by our secrets?

Fear. The fear of rejection, the fear of what the truth might require of us, and the fear of admitting how lost we truly feel.

To say out loud to another human being, "I had an abortion last year" or "My father molested me throughout my childhood" or "I can't stop looking at porn" would bring a reality to the pain that we've buried. If someone else knows, then we can no longer pretend.

When Hope accepted the invitation to come out of hiding, she knew her life was never going to be the same. She couldn't be sure how her blog followers would respond to her post or if her husband would forgive and embrace her after he knew her secrets. There was no guarantee that she would find freedom from her shame. She just knew that her secrets were holding her captive.

You Can't Heal in Hiding

Who do you think was more invested in Hope's silence about her abuse and struggle? Satan or God? Who whispered, "They'll never accept you if they know!" And who invited Hope to step into truth instead of harboring her secrets?

God is not the one telling us to hide. He understands our shame and fear. He is a gentleman, not demanding that we tell our secrets but inviting us to trust Him in the light. Jesus came to this earth to set us free: free from shame, free from the bondage of sin, and free from the power of our secrets.

The enemy knows that healing doesn't come in darkness but instead when we step into the light. He desperately wants us to be bound by secrets. When Hope was silent, the enemy was winning.

She determined, "I have to quit hiding from myself . . . from God. Right here. Right now. And pursue my healing, the healing I so desperately seek and long for."

While secrets have power, stepping into the truth can be life-changing. The two of us have had the privilege of being the person to whom women have first spoken some of their secrets. Secrets of an affair. Secrets of an addiction. Secrets of a shameful trauma. Secrets of a fantasy life no one knows about. When the words are whispered through tears and fear, a ray of light appears—light that gives hope.

No Intimacy without Honesty

Intimacy in relationships can only go as far as honesty. The average couple may pledge "my whole self to you," but in reality most of us give only a percentage of who we are to our spouses. Only the crucible of time, trials, and conflict compels us to begin exposing our secrets.

Hope and her husband had been married for many years. They regularly had sex, raised their children, and ran a household together, yet they did not have intimacy because they were not honest with each other about how they felt and who they were.

In a later blog post Hope wrote:

We were two friends with benefits and responsibilities. There was no intimacy. No sharing our lives. No connection.

No love ... at least not a passionate, romantic love. When I finally came to the end of myself, admitted who I was and was not and was willing to lay my soul bare before Abba and my husband, healing became possible. I'm a lot more honest about things now. My husband is honest too. We don't let each other get away with hiding from one another. Even though it hurts, we continue to talk through the last twenty years. I tell him if I like or don't like something. I'm honest about words, situations, and songs that will trigger me. I let him see me falling apart, knowing that when I'm weak he is strong. He is learning that I can deal with his weakness and be strong for him. Being honest has increased intimacy and improved our marriage.

Does your most intimate relationship feel superficial? You can be married, living in the same house, sleeping in the same bed, and still be hiding from each other. The covenant of marriage invites you to share your secrets rather than hiding from them. There is no intimacy in hide-and-seek until you learn to hide together.

How Do I Stop Hiding?

Journalist Dorothy Dix reportedly wrote, "Confession is always weakness. The brave soul keeps its own secrets, and takes its own punishment in silence."[1] What a tragic way to live life! Before sharing her secrets with another person, Hope first came out of hiding with the Lord, the One who already knew them.

Isn't it crazy that we think we can hide from God? Growing up I (Juli) had a little, white dog, Amanda, who really wanted to please us. Whenever she did something wrong, she hid. The problem was, she hid by sticking her head under the couch while her entire backside was still in perfect view. I suppose her little doggy brain thought if she couldn't see us, then we couldn't see her.

Isn't this just how we hide from God? We believe that if He isn't in our thoughts, then we must not be in His. God not only knows every thought you've ever had, He understands why you act the way you do. Read Psalm 139 and you'll be shaking your head in agreement with David, "I can never escape from your Spirit! I can never get away from your presence!" (Psalm 139:7 NLT).

David, who had an incredible relationship with God, kept secrets for a time. It literally made him sick. Here is what he wrote about his secrets and the healing he found in confession:

> *Blessed in the one whose transgressions are forgiven, whose sins are covered. Blessed is the one whose sin the Lord does not count against them and in whose spirit is no deceit.*
>
> *When I kept silent, my bones wasted away through my groaning all day long. For day and night your hand was heavy on me; my strength was sapped as in the heat of summer.*
>
> *Then I acknowledged my sin to you and did not cover up my iniquity. I said, "I will confess my transgressions to the Lord."*
>
> *And you forgave the guilt of my sin.* (Psalm 32:1–5)

David then encourages each of us to take the same step: "Let all the faithful pray to you while you may be found" (Psalm 32:6). In other words, *now* is the time to surrender your secrets. Don't give the enemy one more day to keep you in bondage to them!

If you run to God instead of hiding *from* Him, God's incredible, intimate knowledge of you can turn from a frightful thought to a comforting reality. He already knows your secret. Will you trust Him by speaking it out loud to Him? Hope heard the gentle voice of the Healer inviting her to come out of hiding and trust Him with her secret, a secret she wouldn't tell anyone. God is inviting you, just as He invited Hope: "Heal. Baby girl . . . there's healing here if you'll just let Me."

Ollie, Ollie oxen free! It's time to come out of hiding.

4

Lorraine's Story

Walking in Forgiveness

*I*t was winter, 2001. Peter's strong arms held me as we lay beneath the white sheet on the mattress in front of the fireplace. Flames danced on the ceiling and walls of the living room like angelic spirits. We'd shut off all the house lights, shut out the world. In this moment, only the two of us existed.

We'd been married for twenty-one years and never, in all of those years, had I experienced such exhilaration and freedom in our lovemaking.

Joy welled up in my chest and spilled out in a stream of unspoken praise: *Oh God, this beauty we share is so exquisite it makes my soul ache. Your unseen hand engulfs us, blesses us. Our love makes You smile, God—the intensity of the passion, the oneness we share. This is a gift from You to us. I feel so close to Peter that I don't know where I end and he begins.*

A tear of joy slid down my cheek and dropped on Peter's bare chest where my head lay. Peter felt the cool moisture.

"Honey, you're crying! Is something wrong?"

"No, nothing's wrong," I said softly. "I'm crying because I'm happy."

Peter hugged me. He was happy too. I wondered, *Could he feel it—could he sense the newfound freedom exploding inside me?*

Lord, You forgave me years ago for what I did but it wasn't until tonight that I finally forgave myself. I refused to let myself off the hook. I punished myself by not allowing myself to fully enjoy sex because sex was where I'd blown it. How stupid! Why didn't I see that in punishing me I also punished Peter? But tonight, I did it, God. I let myself off the hook and I'm not crawling back on that hook ever, ever, ever again!

I'm free! I'm free! My heart soared.

God had forgiven me years ago. Why had I waited all this time to forgive myself?

Spring 1979

Eight women, several of them mere girls, crowded the waiting room at the clinic. Presumably we were here for the same reason: to get an abortion.

A leggy blonde who didn't look old enough to drive hovered over a magazine with her friend, giggling. I wanted to shake them both and yell, "Stop laughing! There should be no laughter in this room. This is serious business. We're all about to do something that's going to change our lives forever."

Nervous and on edge, I stood up and walked over to a tall window that overlooked a busy freeway. I watched the cars go up and down the streets—cars filled with people on their way to do ordinary errands and work at ordinary jobs on what appeared to be an ordinary day. But this was no ordinary day. A few moments earlier I'd signed a paper giving a nameless doctor permission to suck my baby from my womb.

A nurse entered the room and called a name. The leggy blonde bounced out of her seat like she'd done this many times before. She followed the nurse down the hall where they disappeared behind a solid gray door.

What goes on behind that door? I shuddered.

I could not know the emotional consequences I'd suffer in the future because I'd signed up for this abortion; I was only aware of the physical consequences of being pregnant—and *not* married. My grandfather's face flashed before me. He'd be appalled. Me? His cherished granddaughter—his pride and joy—pregnant? I remembered the scornful words he'd spoken when a neighbor girl had gotten pregnant at age fifteen. "Don't ever let that happen to you, Lorraine," he'd said with such vehemence that it shook me. The memory of that warning made signing the consent form easier. Even though I was out of college and a young adult, I couldn't bear to disappoint my grandfather.

On the other hand, I couldn't bear to disappoint God either. I'd been a Christian for five years but I didn't know what, if anything, the Bible said about abortion. Still, I doubted the procedure had God's stamp of approval. People told me not to worry, at this early stage I was only dealing with a "blob of tissue," not a baby. Better to remove the tissue before it became a baby, I figured. I wasn't sure I could go through with this if it was a real baby.

I clenched and unclenched my sweaty palms. *I'm going to do this, God. I'm certain You don't approve, but I'm doing it anyway. I've made up my mind and You're not going to change it.* Then, with tears, I added a heartfelt plea: *Please, God. Don't hate me.*

A nurse entered the room and called my name.

It was my turn to follow her down the hall and disappear behind the gray door.

Thirty minutes later, after the procedure was over, I found myself groggy, lying on a hard rollaway bed. I was not the only one in the room. Four other girls also lay on beds recovering from their "procedure." One girl cried softly. Another moaned in pain.

Cramps ripped across my abdomen. My pain quickly morphed into anger. *How could I have been so stupid? Why did I let this happen? Why did he keep pushing and pushing me to have sex when I'd told him no? Why had I finally given in?* The first thing I'd do when I got home would be to tell my boyfriend that I never wanted to see him again, that I wanted him out of my life forever. Another cramp seized me. I vowed: *I hate men! I'm never going to have anything to do with them ever again—they are such jerks!*

Four months later I broke that vow.

Fall 1979

Peter asked me to go to a concert with him. I said yes because what I knew about him impressed me. He played guitar and led worship at our church. He was enrolled in Bible school with thoughts of entering seminary.

We quickly found much in common. We shared a love for music (we began to lead worship together) and a love for teaching (we became leaders for our small group Bible study). The spiritual connection between us was electric. I knew that he was a virgin and that he was saving himself for the one he would marry. He knew a few things about me as well, but what he *didn't* know could hurt him. He saw me as a devoted Christian girl who could do no wrong. We'd been dating for three months and getting more serious by the day. It was time he knew the truth.

I paced back and forth in front of the couch where Peter sat.

"Lorraine, what's wrong? Why are you so edgy?" he asked.

"I've got to tell you something . . . something I don't want to tell you . . . but you really need to know because if I don't tell you, I'm not being fair to you," I stammered.

"Lorraine, you can tell me anything, you should know that by now." I thought about the late night talks in which we'd discussed our upbringing, our favorite authors, our dreams for the future . . . everything except my sexual past.

"No, not this. This is too hard, too awful." I continued pacing. "You don't know me. You really don't know who I am, what I've done."

Peter grabbed my hand and pulled me down onto the couch to sit beside him. "It can't be that bad, Lorraine. Just tell me."

I inhaled deeply and mustered up the courage to say the words to this good man, this godly man, who had high moral standards for the women he dated. I knew I was not one of those women, even though he thought I was. I also knew what I would say next would shatter his image of me forever. I plunged forward anyway.

"First of all, I'm not a virgin."

Silence. He didn't appear surprised but it was hard to tell because he didn't say anything. I closed my eyes and willed the next words to come out of my mouth because he didn't deserve to be deceived any longer.

"And not only that, six months ago, I had an abortion."

That had to surprise him! My abortion was so recent. Still, he said nothing. The seconds ticked slowly by and he remained silent. What was he thinking? Was he trying to find the words to tell me that I was not his type of girl? Was he trying to figure out how to end our short but intense time together? Was he going to tell me, as I'd told my old boyfriend, to get out of his life?

My stomach churned. Why wasn't he responding?

Finally he spoke. His words came slowly, steady, and deliberately. "Will . . . you . . . marry . . . me?"

Now it was my turn to be silent. I'd just told Peter the worst thing I'd ever done and his response was to ask me to marry him? Was he thinking correctly? I wasn't worthy to be this man's bride. For two months I did not give him my answer, yet he continued to pursue me daily and wait patiently for my reply.

Psalm 32:2–5 says:

Blessed is the one whose sin the Lord does not count against him and in whose spirit is no deceit.

When I kept silent, my bones wasted away through my groaning all day long. For day and night your hand was heavy upon me; my strength was sapped as in the heat of summer.

Then I acknowledged my sin to you and did not cover up my iniquity. I said, "I will confess my transgressions to the Lord." And you forgave the guilt of my sin.

Before I could break my silence with Peter, I had to break my silence with God. I got down on my knees and cried out to Him, *God, I know now that the reason You didn't want me to have sex outside of marriage is because You want my best. Peter is the best thing that's ever happened to me and I didn't wait for him. I'm ashamed, not only because of the sex but because of the abortion.* I inhaled deeply, feeling the weight of my choices. *God, I didn't even talk to You about this abortion, because I wanted my own way. I didn't want to be inconvenienced or bring shame on my family. Lord, have mercy on me. I beg You, my God, to forgive me. Wash me clean. Remove my guilt. Please, please, please make my heart right before You!*

Then it came, a rush, a roaring river of the cleansing power of God as His Holy Spirit thundered through me and forcefully carried away my guilt. Oh, the faithfulness of our God! Oh, the height and depth of His mercy and love! That day I knew God had forgiven me. Like a pure white waterfall, His love poured through me and made me clean!

Peter and I were married eight months later. I stood before him in a white dress feeling like a virgin, pure and new. But as the years progressed in our marriage, I realized that I was inhibited when it came to sex, I just couldn't figure out why. God had forgiven me. Peter had forgiven me, but deep down, I couldn't forgive myself for something—but I wasn't sure what. Twelve years later the "what" was revealed.

January 1992

Peter and I entered church that morning with our two young daughters expecting nothing out of the ordinary. Surprise! Today was Right to Life Sunday. Ushers passed out red roses to the women along with the church bulletin. My heart plummeted as we moved to find our seats. I hated Right to Life Sunday because it was an annual reminder of my abortion.

Suddenly a movie was projected on the large screens over the stage showing an in utero baby suspended in amniotic fluid. The debate over when life began raged strong. Pro-choice supporters argued that life didn't begin until a baby exited the birth canal and breathed on its own, or at a later date in the pregnancy. Right to life proponents argued that life began at conception. When I'd had my abortion ultrasounds were rarely used and the images that could be viewed during the early stages of a pregnancy were fuzzy and distorted—just a "blob of tissue." But recent advances in technology made it possible for the first time to distinguish the details of fetal development, details that were being projected in larger than life form before the church congregation.

The tiny baby that floated on the projection screen was ten weeks old. I'd had my abortion at ten weeks. The baby on the screen waved his hand as if to say, "Hi, Mom."

Bile rose in my throat. I raced out of the sanctuary and headed straight for the women's bathroom. This was the first time I'd come face-to-face with the fact that my abortion had been more than a "termination." It had been a murder.

I stayed in the bathroom until the service ended. I washed my face, pinched my cheeks to bring life back into them, and walked back into the lobby area as if everything was normal. Then I spotted them—a group of five of my friends, two of them pastor's wives, huddled in chairs in a small reception area. Their wilted roses lay scattered carelessly on the table in front of them. I scanned the faces and knew in my spirit the truth.

"You too?" I said to the group. All five nodded. We belonged to a furtive club—the club of female Christian leaders who'd kept their abortions a secret.

After church, I asked Peter to watch the girls for the afternoon. I didn't even object when he took them to a fast-food place for greasy French fries. I went into our bedroom, closed the door, and knelt down on the floor on my hands and knees.

"Oh God, I killed my baby, my child!" I sobbed. "God, I'm sorry, I'm sorry. I didn't know . . . I didn't believe it was a baby. Or if I did know, I didn't want to admit it." Wave upon wave of grief rolled through me. Over and over I told God how sorry I was for what I'd done, that I'd murdered my child. I tried to picture my baby in my mind. I felt a strong knowing in my spirit that the baby was a boy. I talked to him: "I'm so sorry for what I did to you, little one. Please forgive your mommy. I believe with all my heart that you are in heaven with Jesus, that you are surrounded by thousands of children like you who also were not given a choice to live out their years on this earth." I imagined a sea of children, smiling, making dandelion chains and bouncing through fields of flowers.

I wept for a solid two hours. Then suddenly the tears stopped. Nothing remained in me to cry out. I crawled onto the bed and fell into a deep sleep, utterly exhausted and completely at peace.

When I awoke I realized something was different. It was as if I had the word *forgiven* stamped on my forehead. This was the instant freedom that came to me, a surge of solid hope, a true healing by God that sprang up in my heart like a tiny seedling. I experienced the truth in Isaiah 43:18–19: "Forget the former things; do not dwell on the past. See, I am doing a new thing! Now it springs up; do you not perceive it?"

The tiny seedling of healing grew bigger each year. It spread its roots inside me, slowly growing into what the Bible calls, "oaks of righteousness, a planting of the Lord for the display of his splendor" (Isaiah 61:3). But this newly formed oak did not yet have fruit—it was not yet fully mature. So even though I was passionate about God—who but this great God could heal me, who but this great God could forgive my sin and make me a new creation?—I was not yet completely healed in the area of my sexuality.

The healing of my sexuality was a slow process that involved a series of obedient acts before God. God asked me, "Lorraine, will you dive into My Word and study thoroughly My perspective of sex?" *Yes, Lord, I will.* "Will you write a book about sex—I'll give you a friend to write with you so you won't have to do this alone?" *Yes, Lord, I will.* "Will you stand in front of thousands of women and openly share about your abortion with others?" *Yes, Lord. By Your grace and only in Your power can I do this, but yes, I will.*

And so it happened. Together my dear friend Linda Dillow and I wrote three books on God's perspective of sex and spoke at more than eighty conferences all over the world. I told the story of my terrible choice and God's great healing to hundreds of thousands of women from as far away as Ireland and Hungary.

Women sometimes asked me, "How can you share the same story over and over again? Don't you detach from the emotion of it?" No. God asked a hard thing of me: He asked me to emotionally relive the horror of signing that document for the abortion each time I spoke. And the pain was multiplied a hundredfold because now I signed my name in full awareness that I had allowed the doctor to kill my child, not just remove a blob of tissue. Such agony! On several occasions I begged God, *Couldn't I, just one time, choose life for my baby instead of death?* The answer each time was no.

Like the main character in the film *Groundhog Day*, I had to repeat the decisions and emotions of that day over and over again with the same horrific results. But each time I shared what happened, God was faithful to reveal Himself to others as the Great Forgiver, the Quiet Comforter, the Heavenly Healer.

My abortion was my choice. In essence I'd said, "Not Your will, God, but mine." But that winter evening in 2001, after years of saying, "Not my will God, but yours," God put in place the final piece of my sexual healing.

Present Day

A Christian leader once said to me, "Forgiving yourself is not a biblical principle—you won't find it discussed in the Bible." She added, "Failure to forgive yourself is the pinnacle of arrogance and pride because essentially you are saying that what Christ did on the cross wasn't enough, that your sin is so great, so 'special,' that it can't be erased by His shed blood.'"

In theory, her arguments hold water, but in reality it's a leaky bucket. When women like me admit the true nature of what we have done, the horror of it and what it cost our Savior, we grieve with a sorrow beyond words. We beat ourselves up: *How could I have been so selfish and disobedient as to make Christ die for what I did?* We refuse to forgive ourselves because we don't want to take lightly the reality of our sin. For a time, we feel the need to do something to prove to God how sorry we are, so we subconsciously punish ourselves in some way. In my case, I did not give myself permission to enjoy sex because sex was where my sin began.

But a time comes to let yourself off the hook. A time comes to put away the black clothes of sorrow and put on a colorful robe. A time comes to dance again, to feel again, to embrace life fully and completely.

You Are Invited . . . to Walk in Forgiveness

We are at a conference, speaking to a group of women about God's design for sexuality. As we scan the crowd, we can both see faces streaming with tears. The women crying seem to have little in common. Some look tough, trying to brush away their tears. Others weep openly. Our hearts are heavy because we know why they weep. They long to be free, free from the burden of guilt and shame they've carried for so long. They hear us proclaim that God created sexuality as a beautiful gift, but they have yet to experience its beauty.

As the conference ends, a line forms. Each woman waits her turn to talk, to pray, to confess. Sarah and Keira, Maggie and Janee, Emily and Sophia, Carly and Kate. We can see their pain-filled faces, feel their tears as they sob against our breasts. And each precious woman looks us in the eyes and says, "I know God forgives me. I know I'm forgiven. I know the verses and I believe them, but I'm still not free."

Like Lorraine, these women had asked God for forgiveness, but the truth of it had never filtered down into their hearts. They are not alone. So many women say to us, "I can forgive others; I can accept God's forgiveness, but I just can't forgive myself. What I did was just too horrible." And so they punish themselves to prove to God that they are sorry for their sins. Some become fearful of men or don't want anything to do with femininity. Or they interpret every rejection as a sign that God is punishing them for sins past. Others shut off every sexual feeling, and some, like Lorraine, hang on to guilt, even when God says to delight in sexual intimacy in marriage.

Lorraine thought that by holding on to her guilt she was showing God her deep sorrow. Can you imagine the horror of coming face-to-face with the truth that you murdered your own baby? When the tiny baby waved at Lorraine from the ultrasound, self-hatred seared her being. Her sin was so encompassing, so deep, it affected her on different levels. She says:

> At the SURFACE LEVEL, all I could think was, *I hate sex; I have no sex drive. Why do I have to do this?* At the NEXT LEVEL, I thought, *I had sex before I was married. I knew it was wrong and I'm a terrible person.* At the DEEPEST LEVEL, I told myself, *I murdered my child. Christ had to die for my horrid sin. I failed God.*

How many women live at the surface level, allowing their guilt and shame to wound their sexuality, but never pressing deeper into the truth of who they are?

Jesus extends forgiveness, not for us to tuck it away in a corner but to revel in the freedom of it, even in the bedroom. Dear one, it is time to forgive yourself.

What Does It Mean to Forgive Yourself?

When a Christian speaks of forgiving herself, she is referring to something much deeper than letting go of her past. Our sins are too shameful to forget about and move on with life. They must be dealt with. We intuitively know that there have to be consequences. Jesus died so that *every sin* could be dealt with—abortion, anger, lust, sexual sin, murder—there is no sin beyond the power of Christ's blood shed for us on the cross.

While the world might encourage you to "stop being so hard on yourself," a Christian's understanding of being free from sin is much different. Our freedom is a gift, a debt has been paid on our behalf. In repentance and confession, we receive the amazing gift that Jesus died to give us. We are called to live as new creatures, no longer saddled with the sin of the past.

Dr. R. T. Kendall says of this gift of freedom: "It is accepting God's forgiveness of all our past sins and failures so completely that we equally let ourselves off the hook for our pasts as God Himself has done."[1] It means keeping no record of your own wrongs.

If you ask a group of women, "What is your favorite chapter in the Bible?" many of them will say, "First Corinthians 13." Our hearts respond to love being patient and kind, never jealous or boastful, never arrogant or rude. We want to be loved like this. As we read the "Love Chapter," often we overlook one little verse, a very important verse: Love "keeps no record of wrongs" (verse 5). The Greek word that is translated as "no record" is *logizomai,* which means to reckon or impute.[2] In Romans 4:8 this Greek word is translated this way: "Blessed is the one whose sin the Lord will never count against them."

Do you understand what this means? In God's sight your sin no longer exists. He does not keep a record of your wrongs. Receiving forgiveness means acknowledging the reality that your sins have been paid for. God keeps no record of your wrongs, and He longs *for you* to tear up the mental or actual list you have of your sins.

Lorraine had to tear up her mental list of the record of her wrongs. She said no to the liar when she saw a child the age her child would have been. Instead of going to the list and hating herself, Lorraine thanked God her baby was with Him. When tears flooded her cheeks in the dental chair as the drill brought back memories of the drill used in the abortion, she threw Satan's jeers back in his face by declaring, "Jesus died for my sin. I am forgiven!"

Fighting the Accuser

There is a reason so many Christian women hang on to the guilt of their sin even though they know about God's total forgiveness. There is someone who does not want you to be free; his name is Satan. He does not want God to have the glory shown through the miracle of forgiveness. He would much rather Christians walk in a cloud of shame instead of dancing in freedom and praise.

Not only is Satan called the father of lies, he is also called the accuser. His job description is to make you feel guilty. Revelation 12:10 tells us that Satan accuses us before God day and night. Can you hear his voice accusing you?

Embracing God's forgiveness may be a theological concept, but it can also have practical implications for your daily life. We want to share with you three steps you can take to find freedom from the enemy's accusations.

STEP 1: Recognize the Voice

When you have thoughts that bring on condemnation, can you tell the difference between God's conviction and Satan's accusations? God convicts us of sin for the sake of leading us to freedom. Our enemy taunts for the purpose of keeping us in bondage.

One way to discern the voice of God is to distinguish between guilt and shame. Guilt is related to what we have done; shame speaks condemnation over who we are. When God convicts us, we may feel guilty for our sin, but along with that conviction is the invitation to confess our sin and to embrace the forgiveness Jesus offers. Satan's accusations inevitably lead to shame—an overriding sense of helplessness and oppression. He will convince you that there is no positive way forward and that you can do nothing to be free.

God longs for you to know and receive His forgiveness for your past. Satan wants you to dwell on how bad you are. His flaming arrows (Ephesians 6:16) make you doubt that God could or would completely forgive you. Satan will discourage you with thoughts like these: *What you did was so bad. You can never be a true Christian with a past like yours.* When you discern the condemning voice of your enemy, remember that God would never cover you with shame. His voice always offers freedom. "Where the Spirit of the Lord is, there is freedom" (2 Corinthians 3:17).

STEP 2: Remember the Cross

Satan's accusations feel powerful because in one sense, they ring true. In our sinful state, we are not worthy of fellowship with

God. As the Bible says, we have sinned and fallen short of God's glory (Romans 3:23). If it were not for Jesus' sacrifice on the cross, we would be forever burdened with the condemnation of sin. Satan desperately wants you to forget the cross. He's happy for you to wear one around your neck or hang one in your house, as long as you don't remember that Jesus' death on the cross forever cancelled sin! "Therefore, since we have been justified through faith, we have peace with God through our Lord Jesus Christ" (Romans 5:1).

When she remembered the cross, Lorraine refused to believe the enemy's lies. She responded, "Satan, you are right. I am a murderer, but that isn't how God sees me. I have been cleansed, forgiven, and clothed in the righteousness of my Savior." When Satan accuses you of your past, remind him that your sins have been forgiven by God. You are FREE! You are FORGIVEN!

STEP 3: Declare the Truth

When you feel the sting of accusation and guilt, what do you do? You pull out the enemy's fiery dart and throw it back at him! You refuse to believe his lies and you declare God's truth out loud, "There is no condemnation for me because I'm in Christ Jesus" (paraphrase of Romans 8:1).

In the powerful passage about spiritual warfare, Ephesians 6, we are told to put on the armor of God and then to stand. In fact, we are encouraged "to stand" three times in those few verses (Ephesians 6:11, 13, 14). Holding the shield of faith in our left hand and the sword of the Spirit, which is the Word of God, in our right hand, we stand. And just as Jesus did when Satan tempted Him (Matthew 4), we declare Scripture in response to Satan's taunts: "Satan, you don't want me to forgive other people or myself because you don't want me to be free. You want me to be in bondage. You are not going to outsmart me. I am familiar with your evil schemes."[3]

When guilt whispers condemnation, what do you do? You worship your King, who forgave you and brought you out of darkness into His glorious light. And you sing His praises loudly! When you are refusing and resisting the fiery darts of the enemy, worship is a wall of protection around your soul. So worship, declaring the truth of God's great love for you!

Forgiving yourself may bring about the breakthrough you have been looking for. Your fear of intimacy or determination to stay in control—are they rooted in bondage to the guilt of past sin? How would your life be different if you were truly free?

Love keeps no record of wrongs (1 Corinthians 13:5). Do you believe this? Lorraine said, "A time comes to let yourself off the hook." The name of Lorraine's hook was abortion. What is the name of yours? Will you name your hook and agree with God that it is time to tear up the record of your wrongs? Will you pray:

God, I know I've been trying to prove to You that I am sorry for my sin. You know the name of it. My hook is _____. It is time for me to let myself off the hook. I want to be free to dance!

5

Ann's Story

Taking a Step

When I was eight years old, my mother remarried. I believed that my longing for a real daddy was about to become reality. Instead of a daddy, I got a dark, commanding, authoritarian monster. Living the next ten years with my stepfather created a crisis in my belief in people, love, God, and justice.

To the onlooker, our home appeared to be God-centered. The plaque on our family room wall read, "What does the Lord require of you? To act justly and to love mercy and to walk humbly with your God" (Micah 6:8). My stepfather required me to memorize the Lord's Prayer, the Ten Commandments, the Apostles' Creed, and the Twenty-third Psalm. But after 6 p.m. when shades were drawn and no one could see, he insisted that all of us—him, my mother, and me—walk around without clothes. The man who told me to learn God's truth was cruel, sexually perverse, and evil. I was so confused about what God was like. I was learning these prayers and Scriptures and being beaten and sexually abused all at the same time.

The one light in my life was going to school. I was an A student and loved learning. However, when I was in high school, my parents pulled me out and we moved away. From the ages of sixteen to eighteen, I was locked in my bedroom around the clock. Most days I was given only bread and water to eat. My mother shaved off my hair. My stepfather, in a fit of rage, stabbed my back three times. After barely dressing my wounds, my mother locked me back in my prison.

Because no one in our neighborhood had ever seen me, I was utterly and completely alone in my pain. I had no contact with the outside world. No one knew of my existence behind closed doors.

My mother and stepfather did many, many other things to me, sexual things that are too horrific and graphic to write about. My stepfather's obsessive demands that I be thin and have a perfect body gave me a very warped view of normal body weight. I blamed myself for all the ridicule, beatings, and sexual abuse, telling myself that I was being treated this way because I wasn't lovable.

My mother became more and more embittered toward me. She became physically and sexually violent and blamed me for her problems with my stepfather and for his rage and alcoholism. I had no safe place in my life, no hope of protection, love, and nurture.

Hopelessness and despair were my constant companions. My stepfather told me over and over that the only thing I would be able to do in terms of a job was to use my body for profit, and I believed him. I learned to bury myself into darkness and disassociated from my present world as much as possible. Part of me wanted to die, yet another part wanted to live and to escape this prison. The part that wanted to live is the part that kept me hoping and dreaming for the day I would eventually escape.

Incredibly, the one book left on my bookcase in my dark room was the Bible given to me in third grade Sunday school. Only

God knows why my mother or stepfather didn't take it away from me. Out of my desperation and loneliness, I decided to read the Bible, hiding it under my blankets as I read. The Psalms spoke to me. The cries of the writers echoed many of the cries that had been stifled in my soul. I started to wonder whether there was some truth to their words because they rang so true to my heart. So I put God to the test. I asked Him to prove Himself to me by helping me get out of the house and to free me from the oppression I was living in.

From One Kind of Prison to Another

God answered my prayer through my mother's and stepfather's greed. They wanted me to earn money (so I could give it to them, of course), so I was let out of my prison and taken to and from work every day. The day I got my first paycheck, I found a way to escape. Sadly, I moved in with the wrong group of friends and started drinking, doing drugs, and pushing God to the side.

This was to become my lifestyle for the next year. I had discovered a new way to keep my pain hidden and buried. I acted out in ways that I thought would nurture me and bring me love. Because I was never taught healthy coping skills, I did what came natural to me. God became a distant memory. I was free, so I thought, but the power of the drugs and illicit behavior were entrapping me and holding me in a new prison.

A friend talked me into going to a Christian meeting with her, and a man at the meeting asked to pray over me. During that prayer, something came over me and I felt the flood of tears, a sense of relief, and an overwhelming feeling of God's presence. I had been running from God, and He had chased after me. In that moment, I experienced God in a very personal way.

My life was new, but I still had an uncontrollable internal pull to act out in numbing ways. There was something unsettled deep within me. I experienced a nagging emptiness that nothing could fill. Yes, God was in my life, but I did not know how to embrace His love toward me. I kept trying to measure up, please everyone around me, and coexist with an inner world full of uncertainties, confusion, and lies. Every time I failed, I feared God's rejection.

When I was twenty-three I met Enzo, and we got married. I had wrapped up all my negative feelings and memories in little packages and sealed them shut, and I believed that I was ready for my new future. But then the packages began breaking open and putrid emotions and behaviors surfaced once more. I had constant nightmares and was very emotionally unstable.

If you had asked me what was wrong, I would have blamed my husband for not meeting my emotional needs and not being the spiritual leader in the home. I was in a push-pull relationship with Enzo. I feared abandonment and I feared people. I loved and I hated. I did not trust God in any of this and my faith gave way to anxiety and despair. I started looking to food and alcohol to medicate my pain and to help me cope. I sought out a lay counselor in a church who told me I had to have more faith, to pray more, and to read the Bible more. Even though I now know she had good intentions, her words only heaped on more and more guilt. I felt like a complete failure as a Christian.

Steps of Faith

Even though that first counseling experience was not good, I didn't give up. I refused to accept that I had to be stuck in the pain of my past. I kept seeking help and found a Christian counselor who had training and insight into how I could journey toward wholeness. My healing has been a long healing, yet I can testify to God's faithfulness in the midst of my pain.

My healing has involved my taking some very practical steps. I knew I must do more than memorize a Bible verse, so I asked God to show me how to address the roadblocks and lies. I've been seeing a Christian counselor for years, and as we worked together to uncover my pain and damage, I often asked the Lord for a real-life step of faith that could help me break free from my past. Here are a few of the practical faith steps I took to facilitate my healing.

Burying Barbie

As a young girl, I loved Barbie. I wanted to own the Barbie Dream House, Ken, Midge, Skipper, and lots of outfits for the Barbie family dolls. In my eyes Barbie was perfect. I carried that illusion into my teenage years.

As you read earlier, I also learned some highly negative messages from my mother and stepfather concerning my body. I heard over and over again that overweight girls were disgusting and that I had better maintain a thin and sexy body. I was overly thin and grew up believing that as long as I looked good physically, I would be loved and accepted.

As an adult, I have struggled with my weight and low self-esteem. I was constantly dieting and failing and felt I would never measure up. I was full of self-hate and participated in some very unhealthy behaviors to try to lose weight. In the long run, nothing I tried was successful. The only thing I did achieve was a downward spiral into depression, despair, and self-contempt. I came to a place of such destructive despair that I finally asked God for help.

I began looking up Scriptures and God revealed truth about how HE sees me. I want to share these life-changing Scriptures with you.

- "For as the body without the spirit is dead" (James 2:26). I am more than body parts. My body will not function without my spirit. I have more than one dimension.
- "The Spirit of God has made me; the breath of the Almighty gives me life" (Job 33:4). God created me with the breath of His Spirit. I am not just a physical being— God also created me as a spiritual being.
- "The Spirit you received does not make you slaves, so that you live in fear again; rather, the Spirit you received brought about your adoption to sonship. And by him we cry, 'Abba, Father.' The Spirit himself testifies with our spirit that we are God's children" (Romans 8:15–16). My adoption into God's family did not take place on a physical level but on a spiritual level.
- "Yet a time is coming and has now come when the true worshipers will worship the Father in Spirit and truth, for they are the kind of worshipers the Father seeks. God is spirit, and his worshipers must worship in Spirit and truth" (John 4:23–24). God calls me to worship and commune with Him from my spirit.
- "The Spirit gives life; the flesh counts for nothing. The words I have spoken to you—they are full of the Spirit and life" (John 6:63). My spirit is more valuable to God than my body.
- "The Lord does not look at the things people look at. People look at the outward appearance, but the Lord

looks at the heart" (1 Samuel 16:7). Clearly, God does not define me by what my body looks like. I had been living with a false identity that had been passed down to me. I had held on to it and allowed it to control my emotions and decisions.

⸺⸺⸺

Through these and other Scriptures, God showed me how I had allowed my body image to become an idol in my life. Sadly, I had wasted a lot of time focusing on my body. It was time to repent. I had to bury the idolatrous idea that life is found in having a good figure. I decided to make my new conviction more tangible and bought a new Barbie doll. I dug a hole in one of my flower gardens and buried the Barbie doll deep in the earth. Then I planted a Knock Out rosebush in the soil above the buried doll. It is a reminder to me that I "knocked out" the ideas and illusions of the past and replaced them with God's truth.

Today I weigh well over two hundred pounds. Even though I know God does not judge me by my body, I believe that He has called me to take care of it, so I am working on losing weight and will continue to take care of my body until I go home to Him. What's different is that my body is no longer an obsession. I can stand firm in God's love for me, despite what I look like. God sees me as His beautiful daughter . . . and that is enough for me.

Controlling My Bedroom Thoughts

My thought life has been an ongoing battle in the bedroom. Memories of sexual abuse coupled with memories of past promiscuous behavior can pop up at very inopportune times. The enemy uses these intrusive thoughts to distract, shame, or accuse me. These thoughts disrupt me and take a toll on me emotionally during special intimacy times with my husband.

I desire to give myself to Enzo physically, spiritually, and emotionally. Do you know how hard it is to be abandoned during intimacy when painful images from your past flood your mind? Even when I don't think it is noticeable, Enzo can sometimes tell if I am distracted by my thoughts rather than being present with him.

I find that the harder I try *not* to focus on these thoughts, the more they consume me. That is why I have to take practical, proactive steps to control my thoughts.

Here are some of the tools that I use to help keep me focused on my husband.

- I open my eyes to look at my husband's face. It is affirming to me that I am with the man I love, not a dark memory that causes me pain.
- If it is dark, I may turn on the light. This helps me to focus on the here and now.
- I talk to Enzo in loving ways; I say his name out loud.
- I thank God for the gift of my husband.

There is no magic formula for keeping my memories at bay. I have had to be proactive and patient. Healing from trauma takes time. Frankly, sometimes it would be much easier for me not to have sex than it is to fight the dark and painful images that pop up uninvited.

God has called me to purity and intimacy in my role as Enzo's wife. As I make the choice to go in God's direction, I find that the power of the memories decrease a little at a time. Now when I struggle in this area, rather than personalizing it and looking down on myself as a loathsome person, I recognize it as an attack from the enemy to disrupt intimacy with my husband. That in itself is freeing. The enemy may think he can win in this area, but "greater is he that is in you, than he that is in the world" (1 John 4:4 KJV).

Treasuring My Scars

After ten years of emotional, physical, and sexual abuse, I have many seen and unseen scars. These scars have brought me much pain but, believe it or not, they have also brought me a sense of reassurance and purpose. Sounds crazy, doesn't it?

Two of my most prominent physical scars are my disfigured ears. I was born with normal ears but after years of being punched in the head and dragged by my ears, my ears became grossly disfigured.

One of my ears was so misshapen that after several years of denying approval, my insurance company finally agreed to pay for reconstructive surgery. I was so excited! At least one of my ears would look normal again. Unfortunately, the series of surgeries was unsuccessful, so much so that my ear looked even worse than it had before.

After the failed surgeries, I was angry. Why had God answered my prayers that my health insurance would be willing to pay for the surgery and allowed my hopes to be raised—all for naught? I still had the physical deformity, the emotional pain, and now the pain and frustration of failed surgeries. I didn't want to stay angry, so I asked the Lord to show me how to take a step forward in faith. He answered this prayer at a Michael Card concert.

My disfigured ears and my spiritual ears listened intently as Michael performed his song titled "Known by the Scars." He pointed out that Jesus' scars had a purpose. Thomas, Jesus' disciple, did not know who Jesus was after the resurrection until He revealed the scars on His hands and the scar on His side (John 20:25–29). Because of Jesus' scars, there was no denying who He was and what He endured. When Michael Card made this connection, I asked myself, *Could my scars have a purpose? What might it be?*

That night God showed me that my scars are a testimony of the healing that He has done in my life emotionally and spiritually. I have learned so much about God's love and how much He cares for me as His own. I have learned that nothing happens by accident, and that He allows all things to work for His greater purpose. God is using my past to help others who have also been abused. To me, that is a treasure.

My scars have been helpful during the occasional times I have questioned my abuse. I have wondered, *Did the abuse really happen? How could someone who was supposed to nurture you growing up be so cruel? Maybe it was all a dream.* People who knew my mother and stepfather have said to me, "Oh, your stepfather was a nice man; he would never do that." I am thankful that I was able to touch the side of my head, feel the scars, and be reassured that I was not crazy. Scars remind us where we have been, but they do not have to dictate where we are going.

My physical and emotional scars have given me two gifts: a sense of purpose and the reassurance that I did not make up the story of my abuse. Do I still struggle with emotional pain? Yes, of course, and I probably will until I go to my heavenly home. I am now beginning to reexperience physical pain from other serious injuries I endured from the abuse. It is not easy to deal with. One thing I try to remember is this: *When we know God is in our suffering, our wounds and scars become holy.* His presence in all the various parts of my life is my treasure.

You Are Invited to . . . Take a Step

The six o 'clock news sometimes reveals evil that shocks and horrifies. Another gunman takes the lives of schoolchildren, a father murders his two-year-old child, or a celebrity is identified as a child molester. How can people be so cruel and heartless to other human beings?

Horrific abuse doesn't just happen to distant, nameless people. It happens all around us. You could be living in the same neighborhood as an "Ann" and never know it. You might be sitting in church by a man or woman who has dark secrets that will never be exposed. Or perhaps you are the one with wounds from evil things that were done to you.

As we walk with women through the journey of healing, our hearts break to hear stories like Ann's. Not just a few but many. How can there be such evil? How can parents abuse their children? Because Satan is still as evil as he was the day God kicked him out of heaven.

As our understanding of evil has expanded, so has our awareness of God's power to deliver. There is no evil too great for His redemption. We are privileged to know Ann and to call her a dear friend. God's healing in her life is so magnificent that it makes us want to shout "Hallelujah." We rejoice that Ann's story declares the truth the apostle Paul wrote centuries ago, "In all these things we are more than conquerors through him who loved us" (Romans 8:37).

We can learn so much from Ann. Think about the trauma she suffered as a girl and teenager; you've only read a small part of her story and the great evil done to her. We didn't give you the details because we don't want to hurt your heart. As a young adult, Ann acted out of her pain by making choices she deeply regrets. This only added another layer of guilt and shame to her truckload of emotional baggage. It appeared the enemy had his way with Ann. How could she ever be whole?

Have you ever wondered if you could be whole? Perhaps you have concluded that God just can't heal your wounds. You've simply accepted that your emotional life or marriage can never be healthy. We hope that Ann's story of healing has challenged you to consider that the Lord can come with "healing in His wings" for you, just as He has for Ann!

Your Role in Your Healing

Ann relentlessly pursued healing. If she had been alive when Jesus walked the earth, she probably would have followed Him around persistently, pulling His robe, pleading for healing until He noticed her.

Sometimes healing is like a metaphorical surgery. We lie down on the Holy Spirit's operating table and ask Him to make us whole. And then there are seasons when healing seems more like physical therapy, because it requires that we take difficult steps toward wholeness.

As a psychologist, I (Juli) have met many women who have wanted me to "fix" them. They hoped that something I said would somehow erase the pain and dysfunction from the past. Without a doubt, the women who make the most progress in their healing journey are those who take an active role in getting well. The truths you learn from godly counsel and from God's Word will not transform your life until you begin applying them practically, as Ann did.

We see this throughout Scripture. On some occasions, Jesus

walked up to a person and simply said, "Be healed." But most often, His healing came in response to a request for help. In some situations, Jesus asked people to *do something* in response to their healing. Why? Because God is more concerned with our hearts than with our healing. There was no magic power in these actions, but Jesus invited each person to actively demonstrate faith by taking a step toward or in response to healing.

Do you know the story of Naaman, an army commander of a pagan country (2 Kings 5)? Naaman had leprosy, and an Israelite servant girl told Naaman's wife about God's healing power through Elisha. Naaman tracked down Elisha, who told Naaman to do something that sounded just plain crazy. "Go, wash yourself seven times in the Jordan, and your flesh will be restored and you will be cleansed" (2 Kings 5:10). This was not what Naaman wanted. He was angry because he thought the prophet would come out, wave his hand over him, and say the magic words to take away the leprosy. The instructions that Elisha gave seemed ridiculous and were humbling, testing Naaman's faith.

Similarly, God asked Ann to take active steps of obedience; her healing did not "just happen." She actively pursued wholeness for many years, asking the Lord to meet her and endeavoring to apply truth to her life in the most practical ways.

Because the lies of her past so consistently haunt her, Ann wrote the following statement of truth, which she framed and keeps beside her bed.

STATEMENT OF TRUTH

I am no longer a slave to the false illusion that my value comes from a beautiful body. That idolatrous idea has been buried and is no longer a source of life for me. In reality, my value solely comes from Christ and in His unconditional love for me. My outer appearance has no bearing on how He views me. Since my body no longer defines who I am, I accept the fact that I am aging and that my body is changing. I am losing my youthful appearance. I accept the reality of my earthly mortality. I thank God for the gift of this temporary home, and I choose to use it wisely.

Our true self—the self we are becoming in God—is something we receive from God. Any other identity is of our own making and is an illusion.[1]

Genuine self-knowledge begins by looking at God and noticing how God is looking at us. Grounding our knowing of our self in God's knowing of us anchors us in reality. It also anchors us in God.[2]

I have chosen to bury my illusions and embrace reality, to replace my idol with God's loving truth about me. I choose life.

The two of us are humbled by Ann's example. Neither of us has suffered like she has. Yet in our own frustrations and wounds, we are more likely to complain than to act on the powerful truths of God. Ann challenges us with her courage and persistence. She works so hard! How much effort do we put into growing spiritually, emotionally, and sexually?

Asking God to Redeem Your Scars

One of the faith steps Ann took was to view her pain from a different perspective. Her story reminds us that when God heals, it's not as if the pain never happened. Ann still carries scars from the great evil done to her, but God has transformed the meaning of those scars. They no longer define her as a woman in bondage but as a woman whose life tells of the power and majesty of her Healer.

As Ann stated so eloquently: "Scars remind us where we have been, but they do not have to dictate where we are going." Each of us has scars . . . some seen and some unseen. I (Linda) have a scar on my heart from the degrading verbal abuse from my abusive, alcoholic father. I have a scar on my brain from a traumatic brain injury. No one can see my scar. I seem normal (most of the time!), but daily as I force my brain to focus, I am reminded of my scar.

Friend, do you have scars? Do you believe that God can redeem your scars, whether they are from sexual abuse, emotional trauma, or a surgical knife? Perhaps your heart is scarred. The grief of your child's death, the pain of your husband's unfaithfulness, or the words of hate spewed at you by your teen before she ran away. There are as many scars as there are women in the world, too many kinds of pain to count. In this world there is trial and tribulation, but Jesus declared He has overcome this world (John 16:33). Ann invited the Healer into her pain. Have you invited Him into your suffering, regardless of how deep it is? As Ann proclaimed: "When we know God is in our suffering, our wounds and scars become holy. His presence in all the various parts of my life is my treasure."

Imagine yourself in your healing journey. Are you lying on the side of the road, waiting passively for God to heal you, or are you chasing after Him, eager to take difficult steps of faith to experience freedom from the past?

In no way are we suggesting that it is your fault if healing, as you imagine it, doesn't come. But we want you to understand that God is inviting you to participate in your healing. Perhaps the Lord has asked you to take a step of faith to cement truths He is teaching you. Do you need to bury a Barbie or frame a Statement of Truth in your own home? Do you need to view your pain from a different perspective, asking God to show you how to treasure your scars?

Dear friend, accept the Healer's invitation to take a step of faith—whatever it may be—and then get ready to be surprised.

6

Angel's Story

Experiencing Jesus' Radical Love

Seven years ago if you had asked me to describe how I saw myself, I would have said that I was a "crack whore" who didn't deserve love and didn't deserve to live.

If you asked me to describe how I see myself today, I would say "I am redeemed, loved, forgiven, adored, and a new creature." And if you don't believe that Jesus' love can completely change a person's identity, then you haven't heard my story.

Coming Face-to-face with Love

I had a drug addiction, full blown, for twenty-three years and was a prostitute for six of those years. I didn't have a relationship with God, but I knew that He existed and I just wanted His help. I kept asking for it. He answered by putting me in jail. I kept saying, "No, this is not what I'm talking about, God!"

The last time I went to jail was in 2008. I was coming out of a fog from using crack cocaine and alcohol, so I didn't even know how long I had been there when I was told, "Somebody's upstairs for a clergy visit. Some lady wants to talk to you about the Bible." I thought, *Aw, that's great!* I ran up the steps and saw a little, beautiful lady with red hair with a big smile. I remember we talked about Jesus. And from that day, I thought about her every single day for eleven months. I didn't know her name; I couldn't remember it. But I had a pull to know her because she had so much love for me.

That lady had a love for me that I couldn't believe. Here I was, a ragged prostitute, drug addict, and there she was sitting on the other side of the glass with a smile from ear to ear, just happy to be there with a stranger. But she didn't treat me like I was a stranger. She wanted to come and share the love of her Savior with me. That was amazing for me.

When I got out of jail, almost a year later, I told a friend, "I need to find this lady." I tried to describe the woman who had visited me, but I didn't even know her name. My friend had a copy of our local paper and she showed me a photograph. "Is this her?" It was! It was her, right there on the front page of the paper. Along with her picture was an article about her ministry to women like me. Now I had her name: Becky. My friend called me a few days later and said, "Hey, this lady, Becky, has a house across the street from me. She has a meeting every Friday." And that next Friday, I busted through the door and shouted, "Do you remember who I am?" And Becky said, "Yes."

It was like I met Jesus when I met Becky. When I was a child, my grandma read the Bible to me. She bought me one that had pictures, and I believed the stories. I knew they were true, and I knew that Jesus had walked the earth for me. But somewhere I missed the relationship part, and that is what Becky has taught me.

Jesus loved me when I had nothing to give Him. That is why I love Him the way I love Him. When He first came for me, I had no idea how many men I'd been with. It started long before I became a prostitute.

The first time I ever had sex was at fourteen, because I was afraid this guy was gonna leave if I didn't show him I loved him. He said, "If you don't have sex with me, then I'm going to find somebody that loves me." And that fear, which is *not* from God, drew me into an incident that took away all my innocence. At that time, I didn't even realize all that was going on. But afterward I felt shameful and horrible. But I lived by the code of the street: you don't tell anybody you're weak.

So I didn't tell anyone and instead stuffed it alongside all the other harmful things that were happening to me: kids making fun of me about my red hair, my freckles, telling me I was ugly, a freak. I just started wrapping all that stuff up, and those lies became my truth. From that point on, I had sex with almost every boy who paid attention to me. Throughout that time I experienced sex in other sick, twisted ways.

I created a "truth" about sex in my head: I thought I was to use my body to show a man that I loved him, and that I wouldn't be complete if I didn't.

Love Demonstrated

While I was still in jail, Jesus placed another woman in my path. I call her "Happy Woman" because, like Becky, this woman always had a Jesus smile on her face and was always reading the Bible. So I started reading *Basic Instructions Before Leaving Earth* (my name for the Bible), and WOW . . . I mean the words jumped off the pages at me! Jesus died for me—a prostitute. A liar. A drug addict. God literally reached down and touched me—I felt Him touch my shoulders. It was amazing. I was thirty-seven, on a road going nowhere, and through Becky's love, the Happy Woman's smile, and the Bible, Jesus found me and radically changed me.

I got saved and told God I would serve Him wherever. When I got out of jail, I took a job in housekeeping at the place that He told me to work. I came in really ghetto. I'd been on the streets for so long, I didn't know how to be anything else. I didn't like the work, but I'd promised God I'd do whatever He asked. So I worked as if they were paying me millions. One morning I woke up at the transitional house I was living in, and I hit the snooze button for the first time. I was supposed to go to work at 9 a.m., but I always showed up at 7 a.m. That morning I decided to go in at 9. When I got there and pulled around the corner, I discovered that the building had exploded earlier that morning. I knew right then that God had a purpose for my life, and it was huge.

And then God told me, "You're going back to Akron University" and I said, "No, God, they don't want me there. I don't think You know what You're talking about!" He told me it didn't matter what I thought. I just did everything He said, and He opened up the doors at Akron University. I started getting straight As. That was the first time I've ever seen a 4.0 on something that was good. Every other time it was for blowing into an alcohol machine.

God kept putting women in my life to show me His love. I had a teacher at Akron U who sat down at the table and said, "I just love you, Angel." And I was like, WOW, this is a lady with all these degrees, and so professional! I never would have thought that she would say something like that to me. I knew it wasn't me she was drawn to—it was Jesus! People ask me, You know we're made in the image of God, what do you think about that? Well, I think God's got ghetto in Him because He made me in His image!

One thing I want you to know: I've made some bad choices in sobriety but Becky has loved me through them all. She's never pointed her finger at me; she actually had to get me off me because I was my biggest critic. The love she displays, which is from her heart and from Jesus being in her heart, has nurtured wonderful things inside of me.

Love's Fruit

Knowing Jesus' love has helped me learn to love men in healthy ways. Outside of my father, every man I knew was trying to have sex or degrade me. But after I became a Christian, I started meeting men who wanted to have a relationship with me as a friend. I was like "What?" because I thought men were for abuse, sex, and money. I know I've played a role in this too. I haven't been the best person to men either. Because of the anger and the resentment, I've been ugly to men in a lot of ways that I now understand. It's amazing that I now have friends who are men! And they're really my friends; they don't care about anything other than the love of Christ, and they're praying that I'm encouraged to do more and more in the light of Christ. This just gives me God-bumps!

I'm currently going through grief counseling. The first person I talked about with my counselor was a man who brutally raped me. I can't tell you how hard it was to talk about the rape and to deal with all the emotional stuff that came up around it. I hated this man and wanted to do awful things to him. A couple weeks after that session, I went to an Addicts Recovered in Christ (ARC) meeting. I didn't want to go because I thought I looked fat in my clothes that day. God said, "Nuh-uh, you're going." And so, of course, I ran right to the meeting because I knew God had something for me; He wanted me to go.

God doesn't have a still small voice with me, ever. He's very blunt in the things He wants me to do. So I went up to the meeting. The topic was surrender. I was all excited. I thought, *What does God have for me in this topic?* Just then, the guy who brutally raped me and put me in the hospital walked through the door.

Earlier, I had told God, "If You put him in my face, I'll tell him I forgive him." Here was my chance, but I wasn't able to do it when the time came. Immediately, I got angry, and I went into a corner of the room and cried out, *God, help me. I don't want to display the woman that the devil wants me to be. I want to display the woman that You meant for me to be.* Then a woman prayed for me, and I went back to the table, and I did everything God said. He wanted me to stand up and talk. So I got up, and I said, "Please excuse me for my voice. I'm trying to swallow anger that I need to let go of." I read the Scripture He told me to read about just nailing your stuff to the cross. I shared that Jesus came to wash all these things for us, and that He loved me, and that He was showing me healing, and support, and comfort. And when I sat back down, it was like God had reached inside me and ripped all that junk out, all the anger, all the hate, all those things that I thought that I would never change.

I called Becky and said, "You just don't understand everything that's going on! God is great!" In the Word I'm reminded that Jesus said that the well don't need a doctor. The sick do, and He came for the sinners. No matter what your sin looks like, it's sin. He wants to love us all into being the people He put us here to be.

When Jesus was on earth, He was hanging out with people like me. He wasn't at the country clubs or even the churches. He was looking for the lost and for messed-up people like me. If He were here today, He would be looking for me and women like me to save.

Now through Christ I help women who are trapped where I

used to be. I know the loneliness of just being lost and thinking that nobody loves you. It still affects my heart. When God rescued me, I said, "Help me to be humble, and don't let me forget where I've come from." So He put me in the neighborhood I was prostituting in, just to be an example to others that, with Him, all things are possible. I want to be like Becky was to me, carrying Jesus' love to people who don't think anyone could love them.

Some people have asked me, "Angel, would you change anything about your life?" I wouldn't. I know now that people trudging the streets in addiction and people living in suburbs with their noses so high in the air that they don't see anyone below them are all the same people. I used to write people off and believe they were writing me off because we were so different from each other. But God's love . . . I can feel Him sewing me inside, making me the woman that He put me here to be.

You Are Invited to . . . Encounter Jesus' Radical Love

Eric Metaxas, in his excellent book *Miracles*, says, "There is a popular idea in our culture that even if miracles might have happened at some point in the past, in our modern, scientific world they are simply no longer possible."[1] Metaxas takes issue with this statement, and we take issue with it because we know the miracle named Angel!

Angel's transformation into seeing herself as "redeemed, loved, forgiven, adored, new creature" is as much a healing as if she had been healed of cancer. Maybe more so. The radical love of Jesus transformed Angel in a powerful, magnificent way.

If asked, most Christian women would say, "Of course Jesus loves me! Jesus loves me, this I know!" This truth may be the first thing we learn about the Christian faith. How many of us know the song, but haven't discovered the radical love that changed Angel?

In the Gospels, we see glimpses of women like Angel who were known in their communities as sinners. Jesus' love and forgiveness changed the identities of these women. Angel is right: whether we live on the streets or overlooking a country club, we desperately need the power of Jesus' love to change us.

There are many, many women who know the songs, have read the books, and heard the sermons telling of Jesus' love, but have never personally experienced it. They may have fish stickers on their cars and John 3:16 plastered on their walls. Or they may be walking the streets convinced that Jesus died for the "church people" and that His love could never make it to their neighborhood. And so the love of God remains a cliché, a nice thought that has no practical power in their healing.

Oh, how we want you to experience the transforming love of Jesus in your brokenness! The Scriptures that proclaim God's unfailing love are meant to speak of a living, radical truth that applies personally to you. Angel's testimony should not be a rare one; God's great love is so accessible that our world should be filled with dramatic stories that declare, "I once was lost, but now I'm found!"

Three Truths about Jesus' Love

Angel's story demonstrates three things about Jesus' love that may be pivotal to you in your healing journey and to the role you might play in another's introduction to the Healer.

1. Jesus' radical love is revealed through people just like you.

What would you say if a pastor challenged you to make a difference in the world? Not your suburban world but the world of the hood. Becky, a tiny, red-haired woman said yes to this challenge. She was terrified. The thought of walking the streets of the ghetto at 2:00 a.m. scared her speechless. She had no money so all she could afford to do was walk the streets of Akron, Ohio, and pass out yellow smiley face stickers with her phone number that said, "God loves you." She didn't have an eloquent speech or even a hot meal to offer. No building or program. She just showed up with a simple message of God's love.

While God could and sometimes does extend His message of love supernaturally, most often He loves through the arms of a Becky. There are a thousand reasons why Becky shouldn't have visited Angel in jail. Can you hear Becky's thoughts? *I have nothing in common with this street woman. How could I make a difference in this wounded woman's life? Why would she listen to me?* Becky pushed the thoughts away and said, "Okay, God, I'm going. Do Your work!"

Sexual brokenness, by its very definition, happens in relationship. The destructive messages that come from abuse, rejection, and sexual sin haunt a woman in the core of her identity. Whether she is walking the streets or teaching a Bible study, she is convinced that "no one would ever love me if they really knew me. I'm damaged goods." When Becky just loved Angel where she was and as she was, without wanting anything in return, it forced Angel to consider, *If Becky can love me, then just maybe God can too!*

2. Jesus seeks us out without demanding change.

As a wise man once said, "We are not loved because we are worthy; we are worthy because we are loved." Becky wisely didn't march into the prison with judgment or a list of ways Angel needed to change her life. She didn't present Angel with conditions in order to be embraced by Jesus' love.

The Bible says, "While we were still sinners, Christ died for us" (Romans 5:8). If you are under any illusion that you are loved by God because of something you've done or who you are, remember that no one deserves the love of Christ. We were all in our own prison, in a fog of sin, and desperate for love. That's just when Jesus Christ visits us with His grace and mercy. We could never get to Him in our own strength.

One fall day my (Juli's) three boys were out playing in our muddy yard. They came to the door looking like three little pigs covered from head to toe in mud. If it had been a warm day, I would have hosed them down and toweled them off. But the cooler temperatures left me with a dilemma. The only way to get them clean was to get them into the shower, which happened to be on the second story of our house. Between my muddy boys and the bathroom was a staircase with white carpeting. No way these boys would make it upstairs without staining the carpet. Fortunately, my three little piggies were small enough for me to carry them— and that's exactly what I did! I picked each one up, carried him to the bathroom, and put him in the shower.

My muddy-boy dilemma is much like how we perceive the love of Christ. We know we need to be showered off and cleansed of sin, but we're too dirty to approach Him. Oh, how many women stay in their "mud" at the front door their entire lives without knowing the love of Christ Jesus! Jesus stands at the door offering to carry you in your muddy state into His holiness. He takes care of cleaning you up. Your only job is to accept the invitation to run into His arms.

3. Embracing Jesus' radical love always brings change.

While God's love has no conditions, at the same time, it can't help but change you. Angel has been clean from drugs for seven years. Instead of selling her body for sex, she is using her whole being—body, soul, and spirit—to minister to men and women in the very neighborhood where she walked the streets as a prostitute and crack addict. Angel is living out Jesus' radical love. As hard as it was, she chose to forgive a man who brutally raped her. How did these changes happen? Not as a result of Angel's determination to be acceptable to God but because of the power of God's transforming love.

If you were to meet Angel, you would experience a passion for Jesus that can't be contained. Years later, she is still bubbling over with the astonishment that Jesus loves her. She doesn't serve God out of duty but out of a profound realization of His love for her.

The greatest evidence that a person has experienced the love of God is that she will be changed—not perfect but changed. Even if she still struggles with temptation, out of love her desires will be transformed. This is the natural outflow of love.

Who in your life do you truly love? A husband? A child? A parent? The stronger your love, the more you want to please that person. You want to learn what makes your loved one happy and how to tangibly demonstrate the love that overflows in your heart. The same thing happens to us when we encounter Jesus' great love. We will be compelled to love Him, and that love will spill out to others, just as Becky's love poured out over Angel.

This is how God showed his love for us: God sent his only Son into the world so we might live through him. This is the kind of love we are talking about—not that we once upon a time loved God, but that he loved us and sent his Son as

*a sacrifice to clear away our sins and the damage they've
done to our relationship with God. My dear, dear friends, if
God loved us like this, we certainly ought to love each other.*
(1 John 4:10–11 MSG)

If you were to meet Angel, you would think, *Wow, this woman
loves Jesus.* He oozes out of her, smiles through her eyes, embraces
with her words, welcomes with her enthusiastic hug. Angel has
"Jesus loves you" written on her heart. Even more incredible, Angel
has become a "Becky," walking the streets of the ghetto, loving
the broken women there.

Dear friend, Jesus invites you to experience the deep, radical love He has for you. You don't have to live in a ghetto or be
in prison to question God's love for you. Wherever you live, you
may never have known a love without demands. Perhaps you
have been told or shown that you are not loveable. God's love is
different. Humans love conditionally, but God *is* love. There is no
psychological technique or self-help exercise that could possibly
replace the love of Christ in your healing journey. Jesus said that
He came to "proclaim freedom for the prisoners and recovery of
sight for the blind, to set the oppressed free, to proclaim the year of
the Lord's favor" (Luke 4:18–19). May you experience this freedom
as the truth of His unconditional love for you sinks deep into your
bones.

7

Amy's Story

Surrendering to the Power of God to Change You

Have you ever had a friend who seemed to have everything? The successful, handsome man, the fun, hip job, and a fairy-tale life (with a little bit of Jesus on the side)? Well, that was me in my early twenties. Tim and I were the All-American couple.

Tim was a graduate of the United States Naval Academy and began his career as a naval officer when he was twenty-two years old. I graduated with a degree in graphic design and landed a job in my field right out of college. We were living the life, working hard during the week and partying on the weekend.

The veneer on our picture-perfect life began to crack about five years into our marriage when I found sexually related email conversations Tim was having with other women. I knew that my husband looked at naked women regularly and thought this was just normal guy behavior. I thought I was a modern woman by accepting this; in fact, we had *Playboy* sitting on our coffee table in our home. While I was okay with magazines like *Playboy,* what I saw Tim doing on the Internet took it to a whole new level.

My husband is a quiet guy; it was hard for me to engage him in deep conversation, which is what I had always longed for. So to discover him "chatting" with women about what he wanted to do with them sexually was devastating. I confronted him, he apologized, said he was "just looking" and that he wouldn't do it again. I desperately wanted to believe him. Growing up in a nonconfrontational family, I clung to the hope that he really would never do it again.

Two years later, the problem resurfaced. I was supposed to go out of town with some friends for a bachelorette party in Las Vegas. At the last minute my plans changed and I cancelled my trip. Tim was furious that I wasn't going; I couldn't understand why.

I did some snooping and found a picture of him that he was using to solicit women. I was so angry, I just started screaming at him. Again, he apologized and said he was just looking. But then in an overnight bag, I found condoms, which he never used in our marriage. While I was accusing him, I also excused him, making excuses for why he would have condoms. I didn't want to face the truth, even when it was staring me in the face. I later found credit card receipts that explained Tim's anger at my cancelled trip. He had flown a woman into town and put her up in a hotel to have sex with her all weekend. My husband was no longer just looking; he was cheating on me.

Angry, I packed a bag of Tim's clothes and took it down to the naval station where he worked and told him not to come back home.

A week later Tim called me; I could barely make out his voice since he'd been crying so much. He said he was so sorry and asked if we could talk. We talked and then prayed together for the first time in our marriage. I told him he could come back home and we'd work on things slowly, in my time and on my terms. We saw a counselor, talked through our hurts, and put our marriage back together. Unfortunately, it was put together with duct tape that could only hold for so long.

A couple of years later we moved from San Diego to Washington, DC, for Tim's next naval assignment. We'd been there about three weeks when I found a page stuck in my printer's memory: on it a scantily clad woman sat seductively on a motorcycle. Across the top was the word *escort*. "Oh, Lord, not again!" I cried. Part of me just wanted to pretend that I hadn't seen the page; I just wanted a normal marriage with no crisis. But I also believed that God was revealing something to me that I needed to know.

I decided to confront Tim about it. He used the same old excuse, that he was just looking and hadn't done anything. I so desperately wanted to believe him. He told me we would discuss it on Tuesday after work. A long Memorial Day weekend stretched out before us. I'd have to pretend to family and friends that everything was fine while my world seemed to be crashing in. Tim spent a good deal of the weekend in our basement, looking through a book I'd given him about affair-proofing your marriage. I spent a good deal of time thinking about what I was going to do next.

On Tuesday I began looking through Tim's stuff in the basement. With my heart stuck in my throat, I found the handwritten "talking points" he had apparently planned on discussing with me that night. At the top it read:

WHAT I WANT

1. Relationship, marriage with you.
2. Sex with prostitutes every once in a while.

On the second sheet of the notepad, I found pages of women's names, their physical stats, dates, and what he had done with them sexually. It was like something out of Hustler magazine. Disgusting, vile, dirty. I could hardly comprehend what my husband had been doing behind my back for over a year! I felt sick. Exhausted. I knew I couldn't stay. I had to leave.

In a panic I called my mom. She flew out that night to help rescue me from this nightmare. We stayed at a friend's house, but I left a letter to Tim along with my wedding ring on the living room mantel. I wanted to send a clear sign that our marriage was over. When I came back the next day to pack up my belongings, I found a journal entry Tim had left beside our bed. In it he acknowledged our marriage was over and that it was his fault. Even though I knew I was leaving, it hurt to see Tim had given up as well.

Divorce. So final. Where had we gone so wrong? I thought we had worked things out in counseling, but now I knew Tim was too far gone.

My mom drove me home to Nebraska where for three days straight I shook uncontrollably. I felt numb. Listless. I had hardly eaten, slept, or felt anything. My mom suggested I get a massage, and when I did, the floodgates broke. With my head shaking back and forth, I screamed, "It's not my fault! It's not my fault!" over and over until I was spent.

For the first time in my life, God's peace washed over me. I felt His presence and was assured that somehow I was going to make it. It doesn't make sense, but in that moment of peace, I felt compassion for Tim. I knew our marriage was over, but I worried about his soul. He had been my best friend since I was fifteen.

I went to visit his parents and told them what had happened. Seated around their kitchen table, I held hands with his mom and dad, my mom completing the circle. With tears streaming down my cheeks, we prayed for Tim. I begged God to take care of Tim because I knew He was his only hope.

God Does the Impossible

Before God heals a marriage, He begins with each person. God began to rebuild our marriage from the ground up. He started by rebuilding us. I immediately filed for divorce and moved to San Diego to start a new life. Tim was still in DC, a million miles from me. Our ever-present God began working on both coasts.

Three days after I'd arrived in San Diego, I was reading a daily devotion, and the topic was "unclean" people. It would have made sense for me to think of Tim as the unclean person in my life, but that's not what happened. In that moment, God confronted me in my own sin, including my alcohol abuse, my insatiable need for attention (especially from men), and my self-righteousness, to name a few. I realized that God sees my sin the same way that He sees Tim's sin.

That day happened to be our eighth anniversary. I picked up the phone and called Tim; I had no anger, no bitterness. In essence I told him, "I still love you but we can't be married."

A few days later, a friend invited me to her church. There I heard a message on keeping my focus on Jesus. Hot, healing tears flowed down my cheeks. Then I read an announcement in the bulletin about a women's Bible study titled, "Keeping Your Focus When Your Dreams Have Been Shattered." It may have well have said, "Dear Amy, this is for you. Love, God."

With my stomach doing somersaults, I showed up at that Bible study. We were asked to introduce ourselves, and by the time it was my turn, I could hardly breathe. I blurted out my story. I'll always be grateful to the leader, who immediately encouraged the women to place their hands on me and pray for me. I could feel God's love through them. When I asked afterward what I should do now, I was wisely advised that only God had the answer.

In that study, I learned that God allows trials for His higher purposes. I started to have hope that He could work all of this for good, but this Bible study also gave me a hunger for God's Word. I couldn't believe how practical the Bible was and how God spoke to me personally through it. I saw God as He is for the first time. In my superficial Christianity, I thought of God like Santa Claus, a distant cosmic being who wants to make us happy.

I was overwhelmed by both the holiness and grace of the living God. I realized that there was nothing I could do to earn salvation; I had to depend upon grace. I gave my life completely to Jesus.

On the East Coast, God was also working in Tim's heart, confronting him with his sin. He finally began to admit that he had a problem greater than his self-control. He started attending a sexaholic anonymous group, but what really began to transform him was a book by Philip Yancey, *The Jesus I Never Knew*.

I'll let Tim tell you his story in his own words:

As I was reading this book, I realized that Jesus really is the Lord. I also knew that if I wanted to follow Him, I had to give up my life of sin.

I was first introduced to pornography when I was nine years old when I saw a *Playboy* at my grandparents' house. From that day on, porn became my comfort. I believed that I deserved it to deal with the stress I had at work and even in my marriage. With the Internet, my interest and access to sexual things exploded. I never wanted to hurt Amy but felt entitled to having what I wanted.

One night as I was reading about who Jesus is, I

saw clearly that I had two paths. The Lord showed me that I could have my sexual addiction or I could follow Him, but not both. I saw very clearly that the path I was on was quickly leading me to death and darkness, but Jesus offered me life. The love and the grace Jesus extended to me broke me down. I knew I had to believe this; I had to act on it. That was the start of my process of being forgiven and redeemed. I didn't even have a thought of my marriage—I knew it was dead. I just wanted to follow Jesus one step at a time. God gave me a voracious appetite for His Word. I couldn't get enough of God. I wanted to be in church any time the doors were opened and learning everything I could about this Savior who offered me a new life.

God's work in both of our lives began by revealing to us, separately, who God really is—His grace and His holiness. We independently developed a hunger for God's Word and sought His healing personally, not for our marriage. We just wanted to be whole.

From a natural perspective, my marriage to Tim was beyond redemption. His parents, my parents, and our friends had written it off as hopeless. Ironically, the divorce papers I had filed in San Diego got lost in the black hole of the legal system, so Tim and I were never officially divorced.

How the Healer Restored Our Marriage

During my journey of seeking Him, God began to speak to my heart over time that He intended to restore our marriage. I was scared to death at the thought. I'd had hope before only to have it dashed. I didn't trust Tim, but I was learning to trust the Lord and what He was doing in Tim's life.

My first steps toward Tim were all about obedience and trusting God. I moved back to DC to be near Tim. Only three people on the planet were behind this decision: Tim's pastor on the East Coast, my friend on the West Coast, and Tim. By then, he had come to a place of complete repentance. He confessed everything he had done and begged for my forgiveness. He even got down on one knee, proposed, and slipped my wedding ring back on my finger.

This may sound like a romantic scene from a chick flick, but in reality it felt like an invitation to be hurt again. I could see that Tim was different because of what God had done; and I was different—a new creation in Christ—but I had naively hoped that things would be different before, only to see them shatter. How could I know for sure that this wouldn't be a repeat of history?

Before I go any further, I need to tell you that our restoration took fifteen years. God can heal a marriage in an instant, but the long journey of growing and learning to trust again is too valuable to circumvent. The Healer wanted to do more than fix our marriage, He wanted to transform His children.

This has NOT been an easy road. Initially, the thought of being sexually intimate with Tim again made me want to throw up. At times I wanted to start running and never come back.

God asked me to do four things along this journey of rebuilding trust. Although every person and situation is unique, I think these are fairly common steps on the road to healing.

STEP 1: Have an open heart and believe that restoration is possible, even when no one else does

The heart of Christianity is believing that God raised Jesus from the dead, and that He can do the same for us. My marriage was literally dead, yet God asked me to believe that He could resurrect intimacy and the covenant that had been destroyed.

God pointed out to me that the intimacy I so longed for with my husband would never be realized unless I was willing to be vulnerable and real. It's scary to risk being hurt again, but Jesus understands what it's like to be vulnerable and He was with me every step of the way. I had to make the choice to slowly give Tim my heart again.

Having hope is a scary thought, particularly when your hope has been crushed so often in the past. What I realized is that God was asking me to trust Him, not Tim. I believed that God could change my husband—if Tim would let Him—and I saw Him do just that through the power of the Word and the Holy Spirit.

STEP 2: Be willing to forgive

Forgiveness didn't mean letting Tim off the hook. It meant taking him off *my* hook and putting him on God's hook. I had to trust that He would deal with Tim, just as He was dealing with me.

Even if I'd never received an apology from Tim, I still needed to forgive him. Once I understood how much God had forgiven me of, it seemed downright ludicrous to withhold forgiveness from Tim or anyone else.

When I truly forgave Tim, I gave up my right to bring up past sins. I forgave Tim for the things he had done before we were separated, and I've had to forgive him for setbacks after we reconciled.

I also had to understand that forgiveness doesn't mean acting as if the betrayal never happened. A friend taught me a very eye-opening and healthy equation: Forgiveness + Repentance = Relationship.

Because I had forgiven and Tim had repented, God could restore our relationship.

STEP 3: Set loving boundaries

True love doesn't enable sinful or harmful patterns. If I really cared about Tim, I have to have the courage to speak the truth to him in love, even if it hurts. I love him enough to want to help him grow and become more like Christ.

Sometimes I imagine what would have happened if I had accepted Tim's terms for our marriage: a relationship/marriage with me and sex with prostitutes every once in a while. Tim would have gotten what he wanted and we would have both continued toward disaster. Setting boundaries can be painful, but God has used that pain in my life and Tim's to call us both to holy love.

Loving my husband doesn't mean always giving him what he wants or demands. God's love teaches us how to love . . . to always look out for the *best interest* of the other person. God is more interested in strengthening my character than He is about making me happy. Our culture is obsessed with making sure we have everything we want, but only God knows what we need. Out of love, He wants us to become more like Jesus in character—humble and obedient, with the heart of a servant (see Philippians 2:5–8).

STEP 4: Trust the Lord's strength

We can't accomplish God's will in our own strength. Trusting Tim again seemed like an impossible feat. For Tim, overcoming a sexual addiction also seemed hopeless. The only way the impossible has happened in our marriage is because absolutely nothing is too hard for our God. The Healer began our healing when we each trusted Him as our personal Savior and Lord. He then gave us a deep hunger to know the Bible and to obey Him.

There were (and still are) many days of choosing obedience over what we wanted in that moment. But God has been with us through this journey, giving us wisdom and strength when we didn't have it. He is teaching us how to depend upon Him to fight for our marriage.

Where We Are Now

Tim and I now have two children. I want people to see what God can do when you give Him your whole life—the good and the bad. He worked a miracle in our lives. What we are living now is so much more beautiful than either of us imagined marriage could be. With God all things are possible; we are living proof. If God can heal us, He can heal anyone!

You Are Invited . . .
to Surrender to God's Power to Change You

When we asked women what words come to mind when they think of power, the most common responses were *dynamic, explosive,* and *overwhelming.* And this is the way *power* is used in Romans 1:16: "I am not ashamed of the gospel, because it is the *power* of God that brings salvation to everyone who believes." In fact, the Greek word Paul uses here for power is *dunamis.* It's the same root word that gives us English words like *dynamite* and *dynamic.* When dynamite is ignited, the landscape will no longer look the same. This kind of power leaves change in its wake.

We want to ask you a question, a question we ask ourselves. Is the *dunamis* of God evident in your life? Are His Word and presence leaving a wake of change?

If you had met Tim and Amy years ago, they may have told you that they were Christians. This meant they sporadically attended church and had a Bible or two floating around their house. Yet, they both lacked the *dunamis* of God in their lives and marriage. Determination and even counseling didn't make a lasting difference on the sin patterns and addiction that eroded their relationship.

The one and only reason why Tim and Amy have an intimate and healthy relationship today is because they each went beyond their superficial faith of childhood and encountered the risen Savior, Jesus Christ. They met the Healer.

Oh, so many Christians think a relationship with God can be an optional addition to their busy lives. Wilbur Rees wrote a poem called "$3 Worth of God" that describes the underlying attitude of this thinking. It expresses the feelings of someone who wants just enough of God to make him happy but not enough to change him ("I want ecstasy, not transformation"[1]). The *dunamis* of God's Word and presence invades our lives when we dare to ask for more than $3 worth of God—when we dare to seek Him with our whole heart.

Jesus Changes People

Unfortunately, many people believe they know Jesus because they've heard Him described and explained. Yet they have never had a life-changing encounter with the Lord.

When Jesus walked on this earth, He was daily among crowds of people, teaching and extending mercy. We know from Scripture that many people were healed and others became His followers. Yet not *everyone* who was in the same physical space as Jesus was spiritually impacted by His presence. In fact, some of those who crucified Him had been with Him.

People can be exposed to Jesus but not be changed by Him. You may have spent decades sitting in church, attending spiritual retreats, and reading Christian books without encountering the *dunamis* of the Healer. It's not enough to have a polite relationship with Jesus Christ. His healing power comes when we allow His presence to invade our lives.

The apostle Paul was on the way to Damascus to imprison Christians when Jesus invaded his life in a miraculous way. He spoke directly to Paul (then Saul). "Saul, Saul, why are you persecuting me?" (Acts 22:7 NASB). After that encounter, Paul's life took a dramatic turn and instead of fighting against Christians, he gave everything—even his life—for the cause of Christ.

Paul came face-to-face with the power of God in a miraculous way. It is not just in Scripture that we read of men and women who have encountered the dynamite power of God. You have met women in this book who have dynamic, effective lives because they've come face-to-face with God's mighty power and allowed it to change them.

If you could sit down and have coffee with Amy and Tim like we did, you would sense they encountered God's holiness and were turned inside out. We asked Tim, "What made the difference in your life? The Sexaholics Annonymous group you attended? Accountability partners?" Shaking his head, Tim responded, "I saw Jesus for who He is. The light of His holiness and His majesty changed everything in me."

Before Tim encountered Jesus, going to church had been like going to a class. At the Naval Academy he took calculus, Spanish, naval tactics—and on Sundays he "took" church. Going to church made him look good—but he did not allow what he heard to touch his heart. Tim smiled like a Christian as he walked out of church, but he'd never asked Jesus Christ to be his Savior from sin. Through his desperation and brokenness, Tim met the real Jesus, and his life changed dramatically. Saying no to sexual sin was no longer rooted in self-discipline, but emerged from his love for and fear of the almighty God.

Perhaps right now you've stopped reading and are shouting at God, "Zap my husband like you did Tim!" We pray with you that He does. But first, we must ask you, "Have you encountered the holiness and majesty of God? Is His power evident in your life?"

Power in God's Word

Look carefully at the verbs in this verse that describe God's Word.

For the word of God is alive and powerful. It is sharper than the sharpest two-edged sword, cutting between soul and spirit, between joint and marrow. It exposes our innermost thoughts and desires. (Hebrews 4:12 NLT)

Alive. Powerful. Sharper. Cutting. Exposes. We love these strong words. One of the greatest evidences of God's work in our life is the power of His Holy Word. The Holy Spirit is able to take words that were written and inspired thousands of years ago and apply them to our lives as if they were spoken just for us. When Amy surrendered her life to the Lord, He began to speak to her through His Word and it became her daily strength through the most difficult trial of her life. God's Word convicted, encouraged, and instructed Amy.

She began to see that her trial had a higher purpose: Romans 5:3–5 instructed her to rejoice in her problems and trials (having a husband who had sex with prostitutes is a *big* problem), but God says this problem can build endurance, character, and hope in Amy's life. Rejoicing in pain was a difficult choice but this verse has become reality in both Amy's and Tim's lives. God's Word has pierced into the depths of their beings and transformed them into people of character.

Amy also realized that God wanted her to look at *her* heart. Tim's sin was "out there" for all to see, and it was easy for Amy to focus on his problems. But God's Word instructed her to look inside her own heart. God convicted Amy that she needed to change her favorite three-word prayer, *Change HIM, Lord,* into God's favorite three-word prayer, *Change ME, Lord.*

On the other side of the country, the same transformation was happening in Tim's heart as he devoured the Bible and biblical teaching.

Amy:

When Tim and I reconciled six months after filing for divorce, neither one of us could get enough of God's Word. We each studied the Bible individually and eagerly shared what we were learning with each other. We prayed to-gether and sought God's counsel. We joined a couple's Bible study. I joined women's Bible studies where I dug deeply into God's Word, even looking up words in the Greek language so I could understand more fully what the Bible means. The most important part of studying was not just to gain more knowledge but to apply what I'd learned. Many times God's Word challenged me, but I didn't want to do what it said. However, every time I did, whether I felt like it or not, I was blessed and my faith grew. God knows what He's talking about. I used to say I wish God would just tell me what to do and I'd do it. Well, He does! Our instruction manual is His Word, the Bible.

What is so powerful about the Bible? Many who open it find it boring or read it without significant change. It's not the words on the page that can change your life. God's Word becomes powerful when His Spirit pierces it into our hearts.

Surrender Unleashes God's Power!

Read this shocking statement: God doesn't need your help to fix your marriage (or your child or your job or your anything). He doesn't even need your help to heal you. He only needs one thing: *your surrender.*

Amy's faith journey differed from Tim's. She made a decision to receive Christ as her Savior at the age of twelve and knew her sins were forgiven and that she would go to heaven when she died. Tim's betrayals and the help and hope of a women's Bible study woke Amy up from her lukewarm faith. On August 5, 2000, she surrendered her life and Jesus became Lord of all! Radical, dynamic change followed.

Shortly after recording August, 5, 2000, in her Bible as her "I Surrender All" date, Amy, a graphics artist, went to a bar to celebrate the opening of a new .com she was involved with.

Amy:

Looking around the dimly lit bar, I saw the walls were decorated with condoms with the .com logo I had designed. I felt sick. I wanted out. The "new me" didn't fit in the condom environment. As I walked out of the bar, I thought *Total surrender leads to total change.*

The power of God flows in to where the power of self has been abandoned. Tim and Amy independently sought the Lord because they were desperate. Their own solutions had failed. Their own wisdom was insufficient. They each recognized their powerlessness to fix what was broken. This desperation and humility prepared their hearts to surrender to the work of God. They realized that they each needed much more than $3 worth of God!

You don't have to hit rock bottom, like Tim and Amy did, before you surrender your life totally and completely to God. The truth is, we are all in a desperate place. Our desperation is just disguised with busyness, noise, and the illusion of self-sufficiency. We need the mighty power of God, the comfort of His Spirit, and the wisdom of His Word.

How do you surrender? One of the best ways we know is to personalize King David's prayer from the Psalms:

Search me, O God, and know my heart; test me and know my anxious thoughts. Look deep within me, Lord, and point out anything in me that offends You, and lead me along the path of everlasting life. (Psalm 139:23–24 our paraphrase)

In writing about the power of the gospel, Paul wrote: "It is the power of God that brings salvation to everyone *who believes*" (Romans 1:16, italics added). The power of God moves into our life when we place our trust in the authority of Jesus Christ.

One of our favorite authors, Andrew Murray, said it better than we can:

The cause of the weakness of your Christian life is that you want to work it out partly, and to let God help you. And that cannot be. You must come to be utterly helpless, to let God do the work. Some of us want God to give us a little help while we do our best, instead of coming to understand what God wants, and to say, "I can do nothing. God must and will do all." Have you said, "In worship, in work, in sanctification, in obedience to God, I can do nothing of myself, and so my place is to worship God, and to believe that He will work in me every moment"?[2]

While training to become a clinical psychologist, I (Juli) spent many years in school learning about broken relationships, trauma, and healing. I know the techniques of modern psychology, and they can be a significant part of healing. However, there is no psychologist like the Wonderful Counselor. There is no self-help book you could read that is "living and active and sharper than a two-edged sword."

Both of us will testify that our greatest healing and strength has come from being saturated in God's Word and surrendering to the power of the Blessed Holy Spirit. No gift we could give you would equal the knowledge of God's love for you and this invitation to walk in His *dunamis* power!

So . . . where are you, our friend? Are you like Tim, with a Christian veneer but no relationship with Christ as your Savior? Are you like Amy—you know you're a believer in Christ and that you'll go to heaven when you die, but you have not surrendered your life to Jesus?

Wherever you are, humble yourself and embrace Christ as Savior, Lord, Healer of all. He longs for His *dunamis* power to saturate your life, your marriage, your all!

8

Rita's Story

Making Peace
with a Broken Life

I love control. When I'm stressed, my therapy is to deep clean or organize. The world feels right when life is predictable. For most of my young adult life, I believed God was with me in my longing for control. I memorized the verses that assured me that life is fair, that doing good would bring God's blessing, and that all sin deserved justice and punishment.

I had an unspoken arrangement with God. I trusted Christ as my Savior, and believed it was His job to save me from sin *and* anything that robbed me of what I wanted in life. For a while our arrangement appeared to be working. I was married to a successful doctor, had two adorable children, a job I loved, and had just moved into the house of my dreams. We looked like the ideal Christian family, but unknown to me, my husband, Bob, had a long-standing battle with pornography.

Bob's love of porn was greater than his love for me and also his Sunday-only relationship with God. We'd been married sixteen years when he began an affair with a young woman from his office. She eventually left her husband for my husband, and my husband left me for her, and the two bought a condo together.

I remember the day it became obvious to me just how much I had lost. My brother-in-law called and uninvited me to my father-in-law's birthday celebration. I was left to get my children ready to have fun—fun with *her* and those who were no longer my family, people I had known since my sophomore year of high school. Bob and I were not even divorced yet, but I had been cut out, removed, and replaced in one swift operation. Few things in life are more devastating than finding out that someone you once loved has become the object of your hatred. The man who had been my friend was now my enemy.

Four days after our divorce was final, I found myself getting my children ready for their father's wedding. I didn't know what to say to these little ones whose lives were being pulled apart by angry parents. I knew their lives would never be the same. Trust was shattered. Our family was broken. And it was because of Bob and *her*. Yes, she has a name (Amy), but I could barely speak it. How could this woman, fifteen years younger than I (and that was a kick in the you-know-where!), have the right to rear my children, to love my husband, and to live the life that was rightfully mine?

More Devastating News

Determined to get my life back under control, I resolved to move on. I wasn't *that* old; I could find romance again. And I still had a job I loved, teaching science at a Christian school. Work became my topical treatment for pain. Every moment spent concentrating on my job was a moment I was not thinking about my painful divorce and my husband's remarriage.

In the midst of my hectic teaching schedule, I had an appointment for my annual physical. My doctor found a large lump in a bad location. When the results of all the tests came back, the report produced a fear greater than the fear of divorce: "I've got bad news for you. I'm sorry, Rita, it's cancer." I wanted to turn around to look behind me and see who my doctor was talking to. Certainly it must be a mistake. Those words could not be meant for me, yet there he was, still speaking in the low tones of misfortune with compassionate eyes.

As he explained what we would do next—a radical mastectomy, chemotherapy—I shut down. With that one diagnosis, any sense of control over my life was wiped away. I had not yet adjusted to the responsibility of single parenting, bill paying, taking out the trash, or having the oil changed in my car. I was not finished grieving the loss of my family and security. How could I possibly go through cancer treatment alone?

The mastectomy was scheduled for several weeks later. Bob agreed to come and stay the night with the children and take them to school in the morning. He and I sat on the couch and talked for a while after the children went to bed. We both cried. His tears seemed genuine, and I saw the first glimmer of repentance: "Rita, you'll live with physical scars of this surgery for the rest of your life, but I'll live with the emotional scars of guilt for the rest of mine."

His words were kind but they couldn't undo the damage. He was someone else's husband now. In the morning, I was going into surgery, and he was going home to his new wife.

While undergoing chemotherapy, I could not leave the house because of my body's inability to fight infection. That meant I could no longer work to make the pain go away. My usual coping strategies were no longer available to me: no cleaning, no curriculum to write, no ironing, no loud music, nothing to distract me. My children were happy to spend time with their dad and with *her,* where the fun was. The darkness just stayed with me like an unwanted visitor that would never leave. In the empty place of loneliness, it was just me and God

I don't think any of us know what we really believe until what we want is taken away, damaged, or threatened. Loss and pain had exposed the fact that my faith in God and His Word was based more on an arrangement (God was to save me, not only from my sin but from anything that robbed me of what I wanted in life) than on the truth of who God is. Why did God let this happen? What about our deal?

It was over a year before my body began to recover from cancer and the effects of treatment. I went back to work, took care of my children, cared for my terminally ill mother, and went to graduate school. Not long after, my new normal was disrupted again with yet another life-threatening illness. God spared my life a second time, but I faced more surgery, a painful recovery, and the lifelong side effects from my condition: short bowel syndrome.

For the second time in my forties, I spent long, quiet months in recovery. Once again, isolation engulfed me. I didn't simply feel lonely, I felt like I was in exile. Isaiah 45:3 (NLT) ministered to me: "And I will give you treasures hidden in the darkness—secret riches. I will do this so you may know that I am the Lord, the God of Israel, who calls you by name."

Finding the Cure for My Brokenness

During this season, my life was filled with darkness and yet in this quiet, dark stillness a deep, spiritual work was set in motion. Much of the time I was paralyzed by depression. Initially, I could not pray but would cry out the name of Jesus. I begged Him for healing. I had not wanted any of this: the affair, the divorce, the loneliness, single parenthood, two life-threatening illnesses. I wanted my old life back! Slowly I began to realize that while I wanted God to alter my circumstances, He wanted to use them to transform my very soul. While He sometimes intervenes in our lives with the miracle of change, other times He uses the ongoing, unchanged landscape to accomplish His purposes in our lives.

Ironically, an unexpected healing came in the form of my sickness. I began to see God using the isolation of my illness to help me face my disease of sin, at least as much as I could bear at the time. There was nowhere to run, no conversation to hide in, and no task to accomplish. It was just me, and God, and my questions and anger. I didn't want to be a bitter person, but I felt powerless to stop it.

I had worked through some of my bitterness toward Bob, but had seething anger toward his new wife. I had lost all that I loved while Wife #2 reaped the benefits of my hard work. She had my husband, my children, and even my furniture. I was continuing to experience profound loss, while she seemed to be continuing to prosper. My sense of justice could not accept any of this. It felt like she had taken my life away from me.

While studying the Lord's Prayer, I was struck by a command that I had never before noticed:

> *And forgive us our debts, as we also have forgiven our debtors . . . For if you forgive other people when they sin against you, your heavenly Father will also forgive you.* (Matthew 6:12, 14)

I realized that forgiveness was not optional; it was commanded by a loving God who knew that the sin of unforgiveness would destroy me. God's plan was for me to forgive others in the same way He had forgiven me. It was the simple, yet most difficult, gospel truth.

God tells us to love our enemies, but Bob and Amy were my enemies for good reason. How could I love a man who had selfishly broken his covenant, who had hurt our children and destroyed our dreams? And how could I forgive *her*? I had a right to be angry . . . a right to hate. Didn't I?

Healing required the obedience of forgiveness, the death of my sense of justice, and a willingness to accept pain and to release pain. Most of all, it required faith in my Savior to use difficulty to transform my life into something that reflects more of Him. So I took a step toward forgiveness. I made a conscious choice: *I resolved not to live whatever days I had left on earth breeding bitterness, resentment, and anger but rather fighting the good fight to overcome them.*

This battle to overcome is *never* over. Sometimes I trust and obey and sometimes I allow myself to be swallowed by pain, loneliness, and depression. What I have found is that the battle is worth fighting.

Staring death in the face has a way of putting things in perspective. Within seven years, I had faced death twice only to be given another chance at life. I began to grasp the superficial nature of my deal with God and to see that what He offers is far greater than the trinkets we bargain with Him for.

Life is short . . . eternity is long. I want to develop the only part of me that I can take to heaven. Christ in me remakes my character and brings a piece of heaven to earth. If I trust in God's plan for spiritual formation in my life, then there is nothing on earth that can destroy His plan.

The tragedies of life and the sinful choices of others can be devastating, but my response to such things can be even more damaging. How I respond is what forever matters. The truth is, Jesus is the only One who will not betray, abandon, or reject me. In my human condition I will be failed by those who love me—and I will continue to sin against and fail those I love.

As I began to accept my circumstances and my own contribution to them, to trust in the sovereignty of God over all things and rely on His precious promises, it became easier to accept my circumstances. I was beginning, in the tiniest of ways, to understand that if I truly loved God and yielded my desires to Him, He would in His most miraculous of ways bring something good out of *everything*. I began to realize that what happens on earth impacts eternity: my soul and the souls of others. This enabled me to finally begin to forgive.

What about Bob and Amy?

As I walked the difficult forgiveness road, God was also working on Bob's and Amy's hearts to bring healing. I think it is important that you hear directly from each of them about what God did in their lives.

Bob:

I appeared to have it all, including good relationships with our two kids. But outward appearances can hide the truth—all was not well on the inside. I lived under the weight of being solely responsible for setting off what turned out to be a 500-megaton cluster bomb that ripped Rita's and my family apart eighteen years ago.

During the years leading up to our divorce, my Christian life had become a performance treadmill where I dutifully practiced the spiritual disciplines and relied on white-knuckle willpower in order to battle sin and temptation. Christianity had become advice, not good news—and I slowly became crushed under the weight of the dos and don'ts. I eventually came to the conclusion that I could not live up to my moralistic grid. I threw in the towel and simply quit trying. My affair with Amy began three years later.

I hit rock bottom on a sunny afternoon. I suddenly realized that I had no awareness of God's love for me. *None!* I tried in vain to remember what it felt like as a Christian teenager to be assured of His love. That feeling had disappeared without a trace.

News of my adulterous behavior had spread rapidly throughout the Christian community. My sin had offended people. The alienation that resulted was understandable. It never occurred to me to ask, "But wait, didn't Jesus die for sinners?" I simply accepted my position as an outcast. And yet, a few months after Amy and I were married, an older Christian man reached out to me, asking, "Wanna go on a hike?" I figured I had nothing to lose. The tiny bit of grace he extended to me on that trail eventually multiplied and amplified in ways I cannot begin to explain.

I used to think you became a Christian through the gospel and then you moved past all that to sanctify yourself by exerting your free will. Discovering *the transforming power of the gospel* made all the difference, and things began to change on every front—including my relationship with Rita.

A year after that hike, grace was pouring into my life like a flood, freeing me from a fifteen-year addiction to pornography and leading me to desire and enjoy an intimate relationship with God. I was employing the same spiritual disciplines I had used in my legalistic years —but with a new set of motives and expectations. I wasn't doing these disciplines to make God my debtor so He'd have to bless me. I did them because I was already unimaginably blessed in Christ. The healing I've experienced with my second wife is supernatural because it is grace-based. It is an *undeserved* blessing that was purchased with the precious blood of the unblemished Lamb.

Amy:

During the months when Bob and I were having the affair, the only emotion I felt toward Rita was fear. We rarely encountered each other, but I frequently spent time with their children, who were ten and nine years old at the time. Whenever I looked at them, the guilt would become unbearable. I believed I was going to hell for what I did. This is what eventually led me to the cross, right around the time Bob and I were married.

I had never heard the gospel before. I was astonished to learn that someone like me could be saved from the condemnation, guilt, shame, and punishment for my sins. The good news of forgiveness based on Christ's all-sufficient sacrifice began to change my life from the inside out. I started reading the Bible for the first time, but I had no Christian friends outside of Bob.

Shortly after I became a Christian, I began to pray for Rita—and for an opportunity to ask her for forgiveness. It took seven years of waiting and praying for that opportunity to happen. Rita had a major surgery that prevented her from driving her manual transmission sports car for several weeks. When I became aware of this, I offered her my car, which was an automatic. At this point, we were not friends, and it was probably very humbling for her to accept my offer.

Rita's love language is gifts. When she returned my car, she had it detailed and there was a thank-you note and small gift on the passenger seat. Her gift marked a major turning point in our relationship. One small act of kindness was returned with another until we began to feel friendly and comfortable with each other.

Bob and I had two young children when we began sharing *strife-free* holidays together as a blended family. Yes—Rita, Bob, all four kids, and me. My fear of Rita and her anger at me were transformed into mutual compassion for each other. Before long we were sharing beach vacations together. Although forgiveness was clearly implied, I knew I still needed to ask her for it.

That occasion came four years later as my stepdaughter's wedding day approached. Rita, who lived out of town at the time, stayed at our home in order to help with the preparations. After dinner the first night, we had a chance to talk alone and I knew this was the time God had given me to say what I needed to say. The words tumbled out.

"Rita, I am so sorry for all of the pain I caused you." At first Rita brushed it off and tried to change the subject. So I said it again, "Rita, I need to ask for your forgiveness. I am so sorry for the pain I've caused you."

That was a holy moment. We both cried and watched the remaining chains of fear and bitterness fall to the floor. And Rita and I became *true* friends. Six years have passed since then, and we enjoy each other's company every chance we get. There are some in the Christian community who think it's weird when they see us together at Starbucks or sitting together at church. But when you've received so much grace and forgiveness from Jesus Christ, how can you withhold it from one another?

As I mentioned, Bob and I have two children. I know it sounds strange, but we appointed Rita to be their guardian—that means if Bob and I die, *Rita* is the one we have trusted to raise them. By the way, they love Rita with all their hearts. And they know she loves them too. There's only one explanation for this—Jehovah Rapha came and poured divine healing over us.

You Are Invited . . . to Make
Peace with a Broken Life

Rita's story does not have the kind of happy ending that Walt Disney would have scripted for her. She is now in her midfifties, single, and a cancer survivor hindered by chronic health problems. Her life certainly hasn't turned out like she had hoped. Some might wonder, *Where was the Healer when she needed Him?* Oh, the Healer was there, all right! He met Rita in surprising ways, and He still meets her today.

Are you a "Rita" with a broken life? You've called to the Healer, but He hasn't turned the heart of your husband or children. You feel lonely; your hopes for a true love story long gone. Memories of past rejection and betrayal haunt you, convincing you that God passed by your door to help someone else.

We cannot and will not guarantee what the Healer has not promised. Too many women have been told, "Wait long enough and pray hard enough and God will bring you your fairy tale; your Prince Charming is right around the corner!" As Rita's life testifies, God is not Walt Disney. There is no formula of obedience or surrender that can manipulate Him into giving us what we want. He is God, the King of kings, the Lord of lords, the Sovereign of the Universe. He is also the Redeemer, the Healer, and the One who binds up the brokenhearted. His healing may come in an unexpected manner. "'For my thoughts are not your thoughts, neither are your ways my ways,' declares the Lord. 'As the heavens are higher than the earth, so are my ways higher than your ways and my thoughts than your thoughts'" (Isaiah 55:8–9).

Rita bears the scars of brokenness, yet she rejoices. She has made peace with a life that is far from what she dreamed it would be. How did she get there?

The Hard Road to Forgiveness

Making peace with brokenness in life becomes more difficult when the cause of the brokenness has a name—or two names. For Rita, those names were Bob and Amy. They were unquestionably responsible for much of the pain Rita and her children experienced in the wake of broken vows. Rita had the right to be angry. Something more precious than life was taken from her. Yet when God said, "Forgive one another as I have forgiven you" (paraphrase of Ephesians 4:32), He didn't put qualifiers for things that were just too difficult to forgive.

Is there any struggle like the tug-of-war between bitterness and forgiveness? Whenever Rita thought about the pain and agony Bob and Amy had caused her and her children, she boiled inside. Her life was filled with daily reminders of what had been taken from her. She shouldn't have had to go through chemotherapy alone or share parenting time with her children's new stepmom.

When Rita prayed for healing, she never imagined it would come through the road of forgiveness. How many women ask the Healer to work, but at the same time hold on to bitterness for those who caused their pain?

When we are bitter, we keep a mental list (or perhaps a real list) of the offenses against us. First Corinthians 13:5 says that love keeps no record of wrongs. But, oh, we want to keep that record! Justice must be done and we take on justice by keeping our list alive and up-to-date with all the offenses. The truth is we only hurt ourselves when we dwell on what has happened to us and fantasize about what it will be like when "they" get punished. Most terrible of all, we grieve the Holy Spirit of God and this is why we lose our sense of peace.[1]

Scripture tells us that the primary way we grieve the Holy Spirit is by holding tightly to bitterness in our hearts:

> *And do not grieve the Holy Spirit of God, with whom you were sealed for the day of redemption. Get rid of all bitterness, rage, and anger, brawling and slander, along with every form of malice. Be kind and compassionate to one another, forgiving each other, just as in Christ God forgave you.* (Ephesians 4:30–32)

As Christians we say we are to forgive as Jesus forgives. He was the Master teacher about forgiveness, and we are to follow in His steps. Yet many of us who talk the Christian talk have a list of things we secretly feel are unforgiveable. The problem is God's Word does not have such a list.

If you could talk to Rita, she would tell you that forgiving Bob and Amy stretched her beyond anything she thought she could do.

Yet she discovered the truth of what Philip Yancey so beautifully said:

> Forgiveness is the key that unlocks the door of resentment and the handcuffs of hate. Forgiveness breaks the chains of bitterness and the shackles of selfishness. While dying on the cross, Jesus said, "Forgive them"—the Roman soldiers, the religious leaders, the disciples who had fled in darkness, even you and me who have denied him so many times. "Forgive them, for they know not what they do."[2]

God used the Lord's Prayer to show Rita forgiveness was not an option but a commandment.

> *And forgive us our sins as we have forgiven those who sin against us . . . If you forgive [Bob and Amy] who sin against you, your heavenly Father will forgive you.* (Matthew 6:12, 14 NLT)

Rita did not just wake up one morning and think, *Oh, I feel very forgiving today. I'll forgive Bob and Amy.* Usually when we forgive someone who has wounded us deeply, we do not feel forgiving. Forgiveness is not something we *feel*; it is something we *choose*.

Forgiveness is an act of the will. An act of obedience. Keeping a record of wrongs is also an act of the will—a conscious choice *not* to forgive. As you have read Rita's story, has someone come into your mind whom you know you need to forgive or whom you need to ask forgiveness from? While God is the Healer, our willingness to obey is often the open door through which we usher in His miraculous work. Could it be that the Healer is just waiting for you to respond to His invitation to step forward in obedience?

A Broken Deal Doesn't
Have to Mean a Broken Life

Rita wrote:

I don't think any of us know what we really believe until
what we want is taken away, damaged, or threatened. Loss
and pain had exposed the fact that my faith in God and His
Word was based more on an arrangement (God was to save
me, not only from my sin but from anything that robbed me
of what I wanted in life) than on the truth of who God is.
Why did God let this happen? What about our deal?

Rita's honest words reveal a truth that many Christians don't
address until they hit a season of suffering. We love God, but our
love for Him is rooted in what He does for us rather than for who
He is. When our obedience doesn't result in obvious blessing and
healing, we protest. "What about our deal, God? Why do other
people who don't even follow You have a happy family when my life
is in the Dumpster?"

The broken pieces of Rita's life began to take shape when she
stopped asking "Why me?" and began asking "What would You
have me do?"

We see many people in Scripture who had to make peace with
a broken life. Joseph stands out as a righteous man whose life kept
breaking into pieces. When I (Linda) had to come to peace with a
life very different than the one I had planned because of a traumatic
brain injury, these words written by a very wise woman ministered
deeply to me.

Joseph, that magnificent hero, became such because he pushed past the obsession with "why" and dealt instead with "how."

How can I please God?

How can I serve God?

If ever a man had the hostile right to ask "why?" wouldn't it have been Joseph? A favored son. A faithful son. Clean . . . malleable yet strong enough to report the wrongs of his brother . . . when asked to.

Cruelly rejected for his God-oriented dream and for his sterling character. We hear no railing screech of "Why, God?" A simple setting to the task at hand.

The question of Joseph: What is your will here?

The human question is "why?" "Give me all your reasons and then, maybe then I will follow You."

The legitimate question, the one that can be known is "what?"

God's "what" is "Do the task at hand. Live the life you find." And Joseph did it.[3]

If Joseph ever thought he had a deal with God, it was smashed when he was sold into slavery and then smashed again when he was put into prison for doing the right thing. The day came when Joseph had the power to even the score with his brothers who so cruelly set his life on a broken path. Instead, he forgave. How was he able to do it? By trusting that his broken life wasn't really broken at all but was instead part of His sovereign and mysterious plan that "in all things God works for the good of those who love him" (Romans 8:28).

From a human perspective, your life may look like an absolute mess. Perhaps you've made choices that took you out of the will of

God or maybe, like Joseph and like Rita, the evil done by others has shipwrecked your dreams. What is so incredible about the Healer is that He is never taken by surprise. He is able to create a victory out of even the most broken of lives.

A Different Kind of Miracle

Let's just put it out there. It's hard enough to forgive an ex-husband and his lover for breaking up your marriage, but to go on and befriend that same woman, who is now your husband's wife and the stepmother of your children? Talk about a surprising turn of events!

Our good friend Shannon Wexelberg wrote a beautiful song called "A Different Kind of Miracle." We feel that this title perfectly describes Rita's story. The choice she made to yield every piece of her broken life to the Lord, including her anger and bitterness, ushered in a miracle—a different kind of miracle. Only by God's grace and healing could Bob, Rita, and Amy worship in church together and co-teach a divorce recovery class.

During the Cultural Revolution in China, the Communists destroyed many items of great value. Priceless collections of china and porcelain were shattered and buried. These beautiful items were destroyed until creative people realized that broken pieces could become beautiful once again. Shards of destroyed china were gathered and individually set into the tops of wooden or metal boxes and the shard box was born. Sitting on a table in my living room is a shard box I (Linda) bought in China. It is a reminder that our God takes the beautiful, broken pieces of our lives and reshapes, refits, and restores them.

Our gracious Lord is so creative in how He heals and redeems! No one could have predicted that Rita's healings (nor Amy's and

Bob's) would look like it does. Yet the Healer did not waste Rita's surrender, her pain, or her life. He beautifully re-created Rita into a unique masterpiece that speaks of reconciliation and a redeemed life through forgiveness.

Does your life look like a heap of broken shards in the wake of smashed dreams? The Healer invites you to give Him the broken pieces and to watch how creatively He redeems them for His glory and turns them into something beautiful.

9

Kathy's Story

Discovering a
Gift in Your Pain

I snuck into bed, barely moving the covers to avoid arousing my sleeping husband. I breathed a sigh of relief, thinking I had succeeded, but before long Scott rolled over and cradled me against his body. I automatically tensed and soon one tear slipped from my eye.

I was silently crying out, *God, help me! Why can't I be like other women?* Although I tried to go along with my husband's sexual advances, pain and fear once again won this battle. With a sigh of frustration, Scott rolled away, leaving a gap in our marriage bed. His bride of sixteen years couldn't perform the one act that brings such closeness to other couples. I'd failed again. As Scott fell asleep, a flood of tears wet my pillow.

What was wrong with me? How had our marriage come to be filled with so much pain?

For the first seven years of our marriage, we enjoyed a plea-surable sex life and often went on getaways to celebrate our love. We brought our son home from the hospital on our fifth wedding anniversary; soon after I became pregnant with our daughter. We were a happy couple with a good marriage, but after I gave birth to our second child, I experienced postpartum pain during inter-course. I told my doctor about the problem, but he could find noth-ing physically wrong. The severe stinging pain continued and got worse over the next several months. I returned to my doctor, but he said I should just have a glass of wine and relax and then the dis-comfort would go away. But it didn't. My perfectionistic tendencies and shame kept me from telling anyone else, including my hus-band, about the pain I was experiencing. For over two years I hid my pain and tears.

With two toddlers and a full-time job, I felt I was justified in telling Scott that I was too tired for sex. But I couldn't avoid all of his sexual advances. Every attempt at intercourse felt like a viola-tion, and I soon began to fear and avoid sexual intimacy. In time it became difficult to have intercourse at all. It seemed as if my vagina had shrunk and penetration was impossible. Finally, I broke down and told Scott of my pain. He was afraid to hurt me further and for a time, all intimacy stopped.

Repeated visits to the gynecologist revealed no physical cause for my pain. Was I the only woman who suffered this way? I felt so alone.

Words can never express the depth of communication pro-vided by physical intimacy. Sex helps to say "I'm sorry" or "Thank you." It physically expresses "I love you," "We're in this together," or "I think you're beautiful." In our marriage this kind of communica-tion came to a screeching halt and our relationship suffered greatly.

Ironically, physical touch is my main love language, and I was self-sabotaging my ability to feel Scott's love. I avoided intimacy yet I *craved* it and even considered going outside of my marriage to find it. But who would want me, a sexually broken woman with nothing to give in return?

I tried to anesthetize the physical and emotional pain with alcohol, the go-to coping mechanism I had used most of my life. After all, the doctor had prescribed that I drink alcohol to relax! Alcohol did numb me, but it numbed not only the pain but also the joy. I drank mostly in private so no one knew the depth of my dependence on alcohol. After twelve years of suffering with sexual pain and failure, I didn't want to feel. I just wanted to be numb. I wasn't proud of who I was becoming; this wasn't the woman I wanted to be!

The Healer Finds Me

God met me right there. He loved me too much to let me destroy the life He had created. It seemed like everyone I met invited me to church, and after months of declining, I finally gave in. I started attending church, and there I learned about the God who is in the business of healing broken lives and who loves me, every piece of me, not just the parts I was willing to shine up and show to the world. I learned about a Savior who wanted not only to save me from myself but to set me apart for healing.

Thirteen years into our marriage, I accepted Jesus Christ as my Savior. His Word spoke into my life, filled many empty spaces, and eased my divine ache, which was actually a longing for Him.

Yet my failure was still before me. The sexual pain was a burden I didn't feel I could give to God. So much shame and isolation surrounded my sexual problem that I felt I couldn't even discuss it with Him.

I loved Scott but I didn't know how to express it, and we were both frustrated. I loved him so much that I wanted to release him from the nightmare that our marriage had become. Even though I was beginning to learn God's Word, Satan was still working on my thoughts, and the evil one did not want our marriage to succeed. And I was still drinking. I thought alcohol could ease my pain a lot faster than God could.

I admit that I wasn't the best wife and I used church and God as an excuse to be away from our home, which no longer seemed like a safe place. I inwardly desired to be close to Scott, but I feared the emotional and physical pain that was sure to occur with any attempt of sexual penetration. He still wanted to go on romantic getaways, but I would make excuses not to go. My internal failure turned into bitterness, anger, and negativity directed mostly at him. Yet he wouldn't leave me! This man of integrity stayed by my side despite my attempts to sabotage our marriage.

The Name for My Pain

Through God's grace, my new-believer's heart softened to truth and I began sharing painful details of my life with a godly mentor. Despite my stubbornness and determination to manage things on my own, she suggested I see a Christian counselor. Reluctantly, I agreed.

When I began to see Carol, I didn't even tell her about my "little sexual problem" until about ten sessions into therapy. After I tearfully described my symptoms, she said, "You have vaginismus." I remember saying, "Vagi-what?" I was a medical professional and I had never even heard the word! She sent me away that day with the assignment to find out all I could about vaginismus and how the condition is treated.

In clinical terms, vaginismus (vaj-uh-niz-mus) is the involuntary spasm, or tightening, of the pubococcygeus (or PC) muscle, which is the band of muscle that surrounds the opening of the vagina. The spasm is unconscious, meaning a woman does not realize what is happening with her body nor does she cause the tightening to happen on purpose. This constriction of the vaginal opening makes sexual penetration painful and even impossible. Vaginismus is most often the result of misinformation or fear surrounding sex. Fear causes tension, which feeds the pain, which causes increased fear, which creates more tension and pain. As this vicious cycle continues, the spasm of the PC muscle is reinforced, at times causing complete closure of the vagina.[1]

Discovering Hope

I finally had a name for my pain and now I had to do the hard work and take the steps to overcome vaginismus. I had to educate myself about the condition and learn to understand why my body wouldn't respond as I so desperately desired. I was filled with hope when I learned that this condition is highly treatable.

My treatment for vaginismus included a series of physical exercises to desensitize my mind and retrain the vaginal muscles to respond correctly. These exercises brought deep emotional and spiritual pain to the surface.

Continued counseling revealed painful events from my past that caused me to view sex and sin as almost synonymous. The combination of verbal abuse, strict religious teaching, and my family's silence about sex had led to feelings of shame surrounding my sexuality. Due to misconceptions from my childhood, I assumed God and sex did not belong in the same room together. I couldn't even pray about my sexual pain because I felt God didn't care about it. Nothing could be further from the truth!

I began to realize how lies about sex had been deeply ingrained in my mind. Through three main avenues, the Lord began to lift the layers of darkness and speak truth into my life.

1. **A sex book.** *Intimate Issues* by Linda Dillow and Lorraine Pintus became my go-to resource to seek biblical truth about sex. I learned that God's Word has much to say about the beauty of sex, and that He most certainly desires for us to experience healing in this area. I was shocked to find out that God gives me permission to be both sensuous and spiritual, and that sex can be fun and exciting without being associated with shame. I devoured the information in *Intimate Issues* and prayed that God could make these truths a reality in our marriage.

2. **God's Word.** Scripture says that God will never leave us or forsake us (Hebrews 13:5) and there is nothing in parenthesis saying, "except when you close the bedroom door." God wanted me to invite Him into our most intimate moments and to trust every part of my being with His goodness. I read through the Song of Solomon, wanting to make sense of why God would place this erotic love story in the middle of the Bible. In Song of Solomon 5:1 (NASB), there is a scene where Solomon and his bride have just made love on their wedding night. A third "person"—God—appears in the room, extends a benediction over the couple, and says, "Eat . . . drink, and imbibe deeply, O lovers." In our intimate moments, I envisioned the Lord blessing Scott's and my union, and holiness began to replace shame. Romans 12:1 says: "In view of God's mercy, offer your bodies as a living

sacrifice, holy and pleasing to God—this is your true and proper worship." In the midst of my sexual brokenness, this verse spoke to me and allowed me to see that even the act of making love can be an act of worship.

3. **Godly friendships.** Since I had lived as a perfectionist most of my life, vulnerability was not my strong suit. I had friends, but hiding and secrecy fostered surface relationships. As much as I craved intimacy with Scott, I also wanted friendships with women who would love me just as I was. Vaginismus tried to steal my femininity, telling me I was less of a woman. Sometimes I felt like I didn't fit in or belong. I was ashamed to admit my struggles to other women. But God began to bring women into my life who accepted me just as I was and were not afraid to tell me the truth. Through these strong women of God, I learned that it is okay to let others see your weaknesses and to rely on trusted people for help. Through these godly friendships, I was able to reclaim a sense of my femininity that I had been pushing away.

Sexual problems have a way of infiltrating shame so completely that it becomes hard to focus on anything but failure. I lived a life that lacked abundance because I allowed vaginismus to rule my life for far too long. When I realized what was happening with my mind, body, and spirit, I got angry. I had to learn how to fight shame and take back everything the evil one had tried to steal from our marriage and my life. The hardest part of the process was once again surrendering control of my body to my husband and gaining sexual trust and communication with the man I love. By allowing myself to be honest with other people, shame no longer held power and fear fell away as Light illuminated and healed the dark places.

A Season of Restoration

I remember it well. The crisp fall day in a cabin by the Poudre River in Colorado, crying in Scott's arms as I kept repeating, "It doesn't hurt. It doesn't hurt. It doesn't hurt." And then, "Thank You. Thank You. Thank You." I was so grateful for God's healing.

Just three days before this joyous event, I'd cried in a friend's arms as I told her I was leaving Scott because I couldn't do this to him anymore. What a difference a few days can make when God is at work! I thank my friend for giving me hope that day. I thank my husband for sticking with me. And I thank God for guiding my path and helping me persevere through treatment.

Satan wants nothing more than to cause women to keep their vaginismus (or any other sexual condition) a dark secret so that they don't get help and so he can continue to torture them and keep them from living an abundant life in Christ. The evil one's tactics are silence, shame, deception, and distortion—and vaginismus has his fingerprints all over it! But praise God that He broke through with His light to let me see Him as the Healer.

Making It Stick

I wish I could tell you that the Lord swept in, wiped away the pain, and that Scott and I have had no problems since that day . . . but I would be lying. We had two years of pain-free intimacy, and then I began to have sexual pain again, but it felt different this time. Intercourse was tearing the delicate vaginal tissue and I began to experience fear all over again. I was diagnosed with another condition called Lichen Schlerosus (LS). I couldn't believe it! Who has *two* sexual pain problems?

Unlike vaginismus, Lichen Schlerosus is supposedly incurable.

Due to LS, the symptoms of vaginismus started to creep in again. This could have been a devastating blow but because of the lessons I learned through vaginismus, I did not allow the old tapes to start playing in my mind again. I realized that my continued spiritual healing was of far more concern than my physical healing, and I relied on the Lord to determine my worth instead of allowing any condition to tell me who I am.

During the "vaginismus years," Scott said something that relieved me of believing I had to endure pain to be with him intimately. I asked if he would leave me if I could never have sex with him again. He got a bit angry and said, "Don't you understand that I just want to be close to you? We don't have to have intercourse to be intimate." It took me awhile to believe his comment, but we now walk in the fact that penetration is not a requirement for a loving, sexual relationship.

Many couples enjoy sexually wonderful relationships without engaging in intercourse. A woman should never be made to feel abnormal because of the way she creatively expresses her sexuality. In our marriage, it was important to redefine what sex looks like for us.

For fourteen years I had vaginismus, but even more importantly vaginismus had me. I may have Lichen Schlerosus but not for one second will LS have me! I will continue to fight for our intimacy and come before the Lord as the Healer of my body and our marriage.

I will continue to pray these words: *Lord, You have created me to be a unique masterpiece. There is no one else exactly like me and You formed me with intention, purpose, and love. Every part of my body, mind, and soul was crafted by You to work perfectly together, including my most intimate feminine parts. Lord, show me what true healing is from the inside out. Everything You make is good, including me. I praise You for how You designed me. Holy Spirit, help*

*me quiet the voices of self-doubt, condemnation, and fear so that I
can become the woman You created me to be. I choose to honor You
with my healing. Amen.*

You Are Invited . . . to Discover the Gift of Your Pain

Both of us love books. If you come to our homes, you will see
shelves lined with them (which makes moving no fun!). As we
scan the shelves of books, one title makes us laugh: *Ten Books That
Screwed Up the World and Five That Didn't Help.* But another title
makes us think deeply: *Pain: The Gift Nobody Wants.* A warning
goes with this bizarre title: "Life without pain could really hurt
you!" Really? Life without pain causes hurts? Our experience
is exactly the opposite—it is pain in life that causes hurt. Who
wrote this book and thinks pain is a gift? Philip Yancey and Dr.
Paul Brand. Philip Yancey, a bestselling Christian author, you may
know. The late Dr. Brand was a world-renowned hand surgeon and
leprosy specialist given the highest honor, the Surgeon General's
Medallion. This highly decorated, godly man has a startling perspective on pain.

> My thoughts about pain developed over many years as I
> worked with people who suffered from pain and people
> who suffered from the lack of pain. I now regard pain as
> one of the most remarkable design features of the human
> body, and if I could choose one gift for my leprosy patients
> it would be the gift of pain.[2]

Why would Dr. Brand wish for the "gift" of pain? Because he has watched his leprosy patients lose fingers, toes, hands, and feet because they felt no pain. Leprosy is a disease of the skin and nerves that causes anesthesia. Pain causes us to adapt to our environment. A numb foot will prompt you to shift your weight, and a burning hand prompts you to pull your hand away from hot water. When people can't feel the pain of touching a burning stove or bumping into a wall, they do things that cause severe damage to their bodies without even knowing it. Perhaps if we had seen the grief experienced by those who could not feel physical pain, we'd agree with Dr. Brand that pain is a gift.

The gift of pain warns us that something is wrong. There are those with "spiritual leprosy" who never feel the pain of their alienation from God or the impact of their foolish choices. How sadly ironic that their lack of spiritual pain will lead to an everlasting agony!

C. S. Lewis wrote, "Pain insists upon being attended to. God whispers to us in our pleasures, speaks in our consciences, but shouts in our pains. It is his megaphone to rouse a deaf world."[3] Throughout this book, you have read about women, including Kathy, who experienced great pain and sexual brokenness. That very pain has led each one of them to the greatest spiritual blessing . . . intimacy with God.

I (Linda) recently asked Kathy how God had used the years of pain in her life. You may be surprised at her answer as she even used the word *gift*.

Kathy:

Pain was *such* a gift for me. I look at my life and all that it has become and so much of the joy I experience now can be traced directly back to my long battle with pain. I can

Surprised by the Healer

truly say that I prospered tremendously, not in spite of my pain but because of it.

Pain allowed me to see the limitations of my humanity and set me on a journey to search for the power of God. He became my Friend, Daddy, Lover, and King, and the depth of His supremacy became real to me! For many years I asked "Why, God?" but as I grew to trust Him my question changed to "How, God?" and the answers began to be revealed.

In the midst of a painful time, it is hard to believe the promises of God! Romans 8:28 is a tough Scripture: "And we know that in all things God works for the good of those who love him, who have been called according to his purpose." If anyone would have told me in the middle of my fight with vaginismus that God was using this pain for my good, I might have strangled that person! But now as I look at this Scripture, I praise the Holy One for bringing me to Himself, loving me, and using my pain to develop my spiritual gifts and bring me into my calling—helping other women in pain. Solidifying my identity may have been one of the greatest gifts that pain gave me.

Not every woman who experiences pain will someday embrace it as a gift. For some women, fourteen years of pain (as Kathy experienced) would lead to bitterness and resentment. At our ministry, Authentic Intimacy, men and women regularly contact us about their difficult situations. One woman wrote several emails about her situation, which was similar to Kathy's. We each corresponded with her over email, trying to encourage and support her. We even put her in touch with Kathy, yet she was absolutely unwilling to let go of her resentment. Her messages were filled with anger and bitterness. She was convinced that God didn't care about her pain so she was giving up—on God, on sex, on hope. Our hearts ached for her as she refused to receive any comfort.

What a dramatic contrast between this woman's perspective and Kathy's! Their circumstances were similar, but their approaches toward their pain are worlds apart. Even suggesting to this woman that her pain could be a gift would have thrown her into further rage and despair. While pain is a gift, it can destroy you unless the gift is opened. You see, you have a role in determining whether your pain will remain a curse or become a profound gift.

When in Pain, Trust in God's Word

Seeing pain as a gift requires a paradigm shift. It means walking by faith instead of relying exclusively on your current reality. In order to embrace that paradigm shift, you have to be rooted in God's Word, which explains how and why pain is a gift to be opened.

God's Word makes some unbelievable statements about how we are to respond when pain invades our lives. One is found in James 1:2. Get ready for a statement that sounds like the message in Yancey's and Dr. Brand's book.

Consider it all joy . . . when you encounter various trials. (NASB)

Other translations and paraphrases even use the word *gift* in reference to life's difficulties and pain.

Consider it a sheer gift, friends, when tests and challenges come at you from all sides. (MSG)

> *When all kinds of trials and temptations crowd into your*
> *lives, my (sisters), don't resent them as intruders, but wel-*
> *come them as friends!* (Phillips)

Pain as a friend? All joy? A sheer gift? If you are like us, trials feel like intruders, not friends. Joy would be having the sexual pain, porn, betrayal, abuse—ALL PAIN—leave, and the quicker, the better. We count it joy when we escape the pain and trials!

James says to consider it all joy in the midst of pain, which includes sexual pain. But there is a reason he says this. Look at the next verses in James.

> *Consider it pure joy . . . whenever you face trials of many*
> *kinds, because you know that the testing of your faith pro-*
> *duces perseverance. Let perseverance finish its work so that*
> *you may be mature and complete, not lacking anything.*
> (1:2–4)

There is a purpose, a great purpose to pain—becoming like Christ! We are promised the benefit of endurance when we encounter a painful trial. If we invite God to do so, He will use the pain we experience in life to mature us so that our character will look more like Christ's character. So dear friend, think on this. When pain assaults you, you have a choice:

You can clench your fist and fight God, insisting that He does things your way. If this is your choice, you will become angry and bitter. Or you can open your hands and say, "God, I don't understand this pain. It feels unfair but I want to trust You in it. Please use this pain to build endurance in me. I want to be more like Christ."

When in Pain, Go to the God of All Comfort

Listen to this beautiful promise from God's Word:

Praise be to the God and Father of our Lord Jesus Christ, the Father of compassion and the God of all comfort, who comforts us in all our troubles, so that we can comfort those in any trouble with the comfort we ourselves receive from God.
(2 Corinthians 1:3–4)

This is a magnificent promise for you. God is called your merciful Father and the God of all comfort, and He longs to bring comfort to you in your pain.

What a comfort to know our Great High Priest, Jesus, has walked where we have walked! Jesus is not distant and aloof to our pain, He entered into it fully. He is close to the brokenhearted and sensitive to our cares. The Bible tells us that Jesus actually intercedes (or prays) for us at the right hand of the Father (Romans 8:34). When Jesus saw the pain of Kathy's vaginismus, her feelings of failure as a wife, and her failing marriage, He interceded for her. What an incredible thought to imagine that Jesus, Himself, intercedes for us in our pain!

God comforts us but the promise doesn't end there. He desires that the comfort and peace He gives you will spill over onto other women in pain. Oh the joy of watching Him do this in Kathy's life! We were in New Zealand and met Zena, a young woman Kathy had been mentoring over Sykpe. Zena told us that she started working with Kathy because she had not been able to consummate her marriage for three years because of sexual pain. Kathy had taught Zena how her body, soul, and spirit could overcome vaginismus. The comfort God had given Kathy, the answers and help and encouragement

He breathed into her life, spilled over into Zena's life. As she pulled out photos of her three children, Zena told us, "I never thought I would have these blessings. God used Kathy in my life in so many ways."

Every woman you've met in this book has walked through deep pain in her sexuality. But today God is overflowing His comfort and encouragement through each one to many other women!

When in Pain, Cast ALL on Him

First Peter 5:7 says, "Cast all your anxiety on him because he cares for you." God loves us so much that He longs for us to not carry the burden of the pain ourselves but to transfer it from our weak shoulders onto His strong shoulders. Two of our favorite versions of this verse emphasize the beauty of God's promise:

You can throw the whole weight of your anxiety on Him for you are His personal concern. It matters to Him concerning You. (Phillips)

Casting the whole of your care (all your anxieties, all your worries, all your concerns, once and for all) on Him, for He cares for you affectionately and cares about you watchfully. (Amplified)

The Lord Jesus modeled this verse when He was in anguish in the garden of Gethsemane.

Then he said to them, "My soul is overwhelmed with sorrow to the point of death. Stay here and keep watch with me." Going a little farther, he fell with his face to the ground and prayed,

*"My Father, if it is possible, may this cup be taken from me.
Yet not as I will, but as you will."* (Matthew 26:38–39)

Kathy would tell you that there were times during her four-teen-year siege of pain that she felt grieved to the point of death. Perhaps you have been there too. It is a glorious truth to know that God loves you with a deep Father's love, a watchful love. He never sleeps nor slumbers. All night tonight He will stay up watching over you and the ones you love so you can sleep. Whatever your pain—betrayal, abuse, wrong choices, loneliness, illness, or physical pain that makes sexual intimacy difficult or impossible—your Father God longs for you to cast all the pain that is tearing you apart onto Him.

Through the process of casting your pain upon the Lord, you will discover that He, indeed, cares for you! God becomes real and personal when we, by faith, invite Him into the real and personal aspects of our lives.

It's Time to Open the Gift

Dear friend, you may never have considered the deep pain you carry as a gift. This thought is not simply a gimmick to make you feel better about the burdens you carry. It is a truth that each of the women in this book will testify to. God can use your pain as a megaphone . . . as a way of awakening your spiritual hunger and thirst. He can use it to make you more like His Son, Jesus: mature, perfect, and lacking nothing. He can use it to equip you to minister to the many around you who desperately need the comfort of Jesus Christ.

For a moment, picture your pain as an object wrapped in a box. What have you done with that box? Have you kicked it? Shouted at it? Thrown it in the trash? Begged for it to be taken away? Perhaps today is the day that you reach out with trembling fingers to open it.

Lord Jesus, please give me eyes to discover this gift in my pain!

10

Alaine's Story

Living a Transformed Life

A woman is traveling on a narrow road. Up ahead she sees a powerful, roaring lion crouching threateningly close to the path. At first she is afraid. But as she gets closer she realizes that the lion is securely chained and that his chain doesn't reach the road.

I am that woman. I've walked closer to the roaring lion than anyone would ever wish to. And I have seen that the lion is chained.

I want to share some snapshots from my life to show you that God can heal anything and use our wounds to help redeem and heal others.

Learning to Live with the Unexplained[1]

Age 7

I love that picture. The one of the Good Shepherd. It's on the wall of my first grade Sunday school class at the church down in the valley. He is a man, but He doesn't have the wild eyes.

I like Miss Betsy, our teacher, too. She has soft hands, not the farmer-lady-rough hands of my mother. The people at this church don't know about my secrets, about my father's wild eyes. I mustn't tell.

Miss Betsy knows about God. One of His names is the Good Shepherd. Sheep. I like all the animals on our farm, but sheep are quiet animals. They have soft noses too. Miss Betsy tells us all about how the Good Shepherd gathers up His sheep and keeps them safe.

She also tells us something that is very, very important to my little seven-year-old heart: she says that if bad things are happening to you, you can pray and God will keep the bad things from happening. Then she tells us that if we ever are afraid, we can pray that He will help us not to be afraid. I need to know that.

I need to know that, because it's Wednesday. That's Rudy's day. He works with my father and every Wednesday he comes and does things to me that hurt me. I hate it when he comes.

It's Wednesday, and as I think about what the Sunday school teacher said, I pray silently, *Lord, don't let Rudy come. And don't let me be afraid.*

But Rudy comes anyway. And like always, I am terrified.

Hadn't I done what Miss Betsy said to do when something bad was happening? What went wrong?

At that moment, God gives me a wonderful gift: He calls it an unexplained box. His gift to me is the ability to live with the unexplained. He tells me that sometimes the only thing to do is to put the things I don't understand into my unexplained box.

It is enough for now. I had no idea just how often I would need to use my unexplained box over the next decades of my life.

No Longer Afraid[2]

Age 35

The coils of razor wire atop the tall fence are daunting. Each week as I park and go through the front gate, I wonder what the Lord is planning on doing in today's meeting.

My pockets are emptied, my purse searched before I walk through the doorway with the metal detector. I can't bring any books here because the spines might hide knives or other contraband. But I have my handouts with me.

I love coming to the prison each week, and I don't mind the search.

After the quietness of the entrance room and the search area, I am suddenly thrust into a different world.

A few of the prisoners get in my face and try to intimidate me. Eventually we come to the chapel and the guard unlocks the door. I quickly duck inside. The stillness surprises me. It's as though this is a small island of peace, of refreshment, in contrast to the chaos and the danger on the other side of the chapel door.

The women will be coming soon. I walk down the aisle toward the front and lay my papers out in neat piles on the first pew.

Soon I hear the door at the rear open as my eight ladies come in. I have been coming here for a while now, each week, to do one thing: bring them hope.

I've never lived in the shadow of the razor wire, but I have an idea of what these women need to hear, need to know. This time, this place, is decades away from the wickedness of my father and his friends and the abuse I suffered. But that has prepared me for this. My past has taught me that there is a God who is so strong and so willing that He can, as the prophet Joel says, "make up to you for the years that the swarming locust has eaten" (Joel 2:25 NASB).

My ladies need to know the feel of gentle touch as I hug them or put my hand on their arm. Some reject my touch. They are still a stone inside. They will, like others before them, be softened by the Gentle One who wants them to eventually trust Him.

My heart sometimes gets overwhelmed by the awfulness of my ladies' pasts. They tell me of betrayal, of abandonment, of wanting to die. I know. I have been there too.

I love my ladies. They are, in a sense, me. My mind wanders back into my memories, and I see myself as an eleven-year–old. It is the middle of the night. I know that my father is sleeping soundly because of the loud snores that come from his room.

I have a plan. I go to the kitchen and find the biggest knife that I can find in the drawer by the stove. Then I go to his room and stand over him as he sleeps. In my mind I envision what is about to happen, as if a minimovie is playing in my head. I see myself raising the knife and plunging it into his chest. I'm not sure where a person's heart is located, but in my movie I aim for the pocket on his pajamas. I think that will be close enough to stop his heart, to stop him from hurting me ever again.

I snap back from my imaginary movie and raise the knife. But a thought pops into my head that challenges my plan. *If I kill him, I'll go to prison.* I don't know where but I have heard of the bad things that happen to you there, like rape, like being tied down. I have already had enough things like that happen to me. I am frightened of prison. So with these thoughts, I lower my arm and put the knife away in the kitchen drawer before I go back to bed.

Now, looking back, I am amazed at the wisdom of my God to lead me into ministry in the very place of which I was so frightened. I am not afraid of prison now. Nor of the prisoners (my ladies!), nor of the guards. I have a boldness now, a strength that has grown out of my childhood. It grew each time God was my strength when I too was raped or tied down. I know I am one who can bring my ladies hope.

They need to know the only One who sees it all, the only One who can put their lives back together. I have come here to tell them about Him.

The Flower Lady[3]

Age 40

"Why would you care about me? You don't even know me. You don't know anything about me."

The words are from a letter written by a young woman whom I met when she came to the teen mom ministry where I volunteer.

My young friend knows very little about being protected, about having hope. Her hope died long ago. The drug and alcohol-fueled violence in her home had a sexual component to it. She already knew whose baby she was carrying. Or at least she thinks she does. Sometimes daughters become party favors that are passed around from one drunken buddy to the next. But she thinks she knows. It's her father's. So she ran.

Somehow the police brought her to our ministry. She was drunk, so she doesn't remember much about why they picked her up. But she knows that this place is for girls like her who will soon be teen moms. She has about six more weeks to go.

Twenty-four hours before her arrival at our ministry, she was on the streets, making money to live in the only way she knew how. Her world was cardboard boxes, garbage cans, STDs. Now she has a bed, and three meals a day. And lights and toilets and best of all, a shower. She'll take long, warm showers, ones she hopes will clean off the filth that's like a cage around her.

As I read her letter I pray for God to show me what to do. I know that He can remake anybody's life. He's done it for me. I remember being a twelve-year-old mother-to-be. I remember being one again at thirteen. For years my eyes filled with tears as my mind pictured me as a young teen holding each of my two little ones. Both stillborn. Like my young friend, I knew whose babies they were. My father's. One of the worse things about having a troubled past are all the secrets. I kept the secret of my Joel and my Rebekah for many decades. Mostly because of the shame. And the ache inside.

Now, as I pray about how to help the girl's home and my young friend, the Lord gives me my answer. He leads me to order one pink rose every month for each of the girls who will soon hold their *alive* babies in their arms. I understand their shame, their secrets. Maybe they need something they can touch and smell to remind them that they are not worthless. They are beautiful, cherished daughters of the King of kings.

No one can explain the joy I feel when my young friend continues her letter:

> Why do you care about me? You are kind. Just like that God these people are teaching me about. Maybe what they're telling me about Him is true. Maybe He cares too.

God, Where Were You?[4]

Age 47

From the ages of five to thirteen, I was a victim of what I call family trafficking. My father sold me as a prostitute to twelve of his friends. It always happened in our home, away from prying eyes, from those who might help, from those who might care.

Where was God when that innocent little girl with her child-like faith believed that He would stop the footsteps, stop the men, stop the terror? Somehow I've never turned against Him in bitterness, never blamed Him for all the wickedness. There's a story in the Bible about two sisters who don't understand why God didn't prevent their brother's death. As I've read the story, I've always believed that one came with bitterness; the other came worshiping. God gave me the ability to choose the latter.

I've always known that the evil is from the dark side and that awfulness doesn't come from the Light. I know God too well to believe that He joyfully watched me suffer so much. But I also know that He could have stopped it, could have prevented it.

So, I've often wondered, *God, where were You?*

Something prompted me to ask Him again this morning as I was getting ready to go to work. I pulled the comb through my hair and wondered again if He would answer the unanswerable. I brushed my teeth, slipped my papers into my briefcase, and headed for the university. On the way, God answered me. I sensed that He was giving me the understanding that I have asked for all these years. I pulled my car over to the side of the road and listened. His message was clear. Not a voice but a knowing inside in my spirit. He told me four things.

"Every time you prayed, I heard."

How kind of Him to tell me that! I can still remember as a little girl wondering if I had prayed the right way. The Sunday school teacher hadn't said if we were supposed to pray out loud or not. Maybe God hadn't answered, I reasoned, because I didn't pray out loud.

The second thing God told me made lines of tears run down my cheeks.

"Every time you wept, I wept."

So I never was alone with my tears!

He continued, *"There's no way that you with your finite mind can understand why I gave human beings the power to choose either good or evil."*

The fourth thing God said led me to a choice.

"Do you trust Me?"

There beside the road with my car engine still running, I heard from the God who has kept me alive all these years. His boundaries around my enemy haven't been the boundaries I would have chosen. I would have shortened the chain around the neck of the roaring lion that has sought to devour me. But I know God well enough to know that with great thought, with great care, with great love He chained that roaring lion and measured the length of his chain.

Thank You, God, for hanging on to me.

Thank You, God, for keeping me sane.

Thank You, God, for healing me.

Thank You, God, for using my pain to bring hope and healing to others.

You Are Invited . . . to Live a Transformed Life

Have you ever heard a story of a true miracle? Not just what we often call "miraculous"—like a sports team coming back to win a game against the odds—but an event that is absolutely unexplainable without God?

I (Linda) received an email from my friend, Sandy, just this week about a miraculous event in her husband's life. Here are Sandy's words:

Chad recently had surgery to remove remaining parathyroids that were working overtime and causing a variety of health issues. It was a difficult operation because he had a lot of scar tissue from a previous surgery. The surgeon came out of the operating room and explained that due to the difficulty of the surgery he had accidently cut through (and cut out) some of Chad's thyroid. Well, a week and a half later we got a call from the surgeon. He explained that he had sent the part of the thyroid he inadvertently cut out down to pathology and they found a cancerous tumor! Not what we expected to hear! After a month or so of testing, etc., it was concluded that the surgeon had cut out almost half of Chad's thyroid and in doing so had managed to get all of the cancer. How is that for a God intervention? He had Chad's cancer cut out entirely before we even knew it was there! No medical professional we share that story with can believe that this very experienced surgeon accidently cut out half of Chad's thyroid. One even said, "What church do you go to? I want to go there!"

We've known of people who have been healed of physical disease but this is the first time we've heard of God healing someone of cancer before the patient, the doctor, before anyone even knew there was cancer! Our God is an amazing, miracle-working God! And His daughter Alaine is one of His beautiful miracles.

We know the Holocaust-like ordeal this dear woman experienced as a young child, and we know who Alaine is today. She is a walking, breathing miracle.

There is much about her life that you wouldn't know just by reading these snapshots from her story. Were we to put into this book the horrors that Alaine suffered as a child not many would have the heart to keep reading. She journeyed close enough to that roaring lion to feel his breath on her face. Today, at age sixty-five,

Alaine still bears many scars from her torture. She has a brace on her leg, oxygen to help her breathe, and a motorized wheelchair.

Yet if you met Alaine, her physical limitations wouldn't be the first thing you noticed about her. Instead, you would be captivated by a face that radiates joy. She is a woman of peace who shouldn't be. Her eyes and smile speak of her deep love for her Beloved. How does someone who has every reason to complain become a person who is known for her unrelenting joy? Instead of being afraid of the "lion" who tried to devour her, Alaine shouts triumphantly in his face. How does a woman who wasn't loved by a parent or husband pour out such love on others? Where do her joy, courage, and love come from?

Meet a True Transformer

Sometimes we hear a Bible verse so often that we become numb to the profound truth it communicates. So when you read this verse, a verse you may have read many times, please don't shift into neutral and shut your ears. Instead, ask God to open your spiritual ears and listen in a new way. Perhaps even read it aloud to cement the truths in your heart and mind.

Therefore, I urge you, brothers and sisters, in view of God's mercy, to offer your bodies as a living sacrifice, holy and pleasing to God—this is your true and proper worship. Do not conform to the pattern of this world, but be transformed by the renewing of your mind. Then you will be able to test and approve what God's will is—his good, pleasing and perfect will. (Romans 12:1–2)

This one passage written two thousand years ago captures how and why Alaine is an overcomer rather than a victim of the tremendous evil and trauma she suffered. She took to heart the challenge to commit her life to God by transforming her mind with His Word. Yes, there were men and women along her healing journey who loved and counseled her through deep valleys. But Alaine intimately walks with her beloved Lord and loves His Word as much as any person we have ever met.

I (Linda) know Alaine memorized the entire New Testament and all the Psalms (yes, you read that right), not because she told me but because I recognized she was describing herself when she wrote about a woman who had vast portions of God's Word treasured in her heart. I said, "Alaine, that woman is you." For twenty years Alaine consistently spent twenty minutes a day hiding Scripture in her mind and heart. She is living proof that we can be transformed into a new person by changing the way we think!

Alaine's interaction with God's Word has never been passive. In fact, she's written a Bible study in which she directs readers in spiritual workouts intended to get God's Word pressed deep into the heart. Here's her explanation of why we need to work so hard to transform our minds:

Scripture paints a clear picture of the warfare we are all engaged in—a struggle between living a life consistent with the truth of who we are in Christ or living a life based on subtle (and not so subtle) lies and deceptions. Scripture also pinpoints the battlefield: the mind (2 Corinthians 4:4; 11:3)....These battles determine how we live out each day. Our thoughts are the starting points for our actions as well as our reactions.

Is it any wonder, then, that our enemy Satan hurls his well-placed darts not generally at our physical body, or at some external focus. He sends them to the control center of our life—our mind. But God is at work too. Through His Holy Spirit, He plants thoughts in our mind also—truths from His Word. Good thoughts, uplifting thoughts, comforting thoughts, strengthening thoughts, convicting thoughts, life-giving thoughts, encouraging thoughts. We have the bold promise in Romans 12:1–2 that as our mind is renewed, our life will be transformed.[5]

I (Linda) once had a discussion with Alaine that reveals just how new her mind is in all areas. She was teaching a Bible study to married women and they wanted a session on God's view of sexual intimacy in marriage. What did Alaine, a single woman, know? Her only sexual experience had been the horror of being sold by her father to twelve men every week from the time she was five until she was thirteen.

"Here's my study, Linda, about God's perspective on sex. Let me know what you think."

Tears coursed down my cheeks as I read. *God, this is impossible. Alaine sees the beauty, the holiness, the gift of intimate oneness. She gets Your gift of sex! Most Christian wives don't even get it. How? How, God?*

I asked the question but I knew. For years Alaine stood under a thundering waterfall of God's Word as it poured over her, in her, all about her. God's thoughts became her thoughts. She saw as He saw. She loved as He loved. I humbly bowed before my God as I held her Bible study pages and asked that His waterfall pour over me.

Turning Tragedy into Triumph

In Alaine's life we see victory: tragedy turned into triumph. Sometimes we view healing as the removal of pain. We think that when God heals, He will, through medical intervention, miraculous means, or perhaps the passage of time, take away our emotional and physical suffering. God intends to do more than just give us a pain-free life. His desire is for us to be able to say with Paul, "Thanks be to God, who always leads us in triumph in Christ, and manifests through us the sweet aroma of knowledge of Him in every place" (2 Corinthians 2:14 NASB). Alaine is a living, breathing aroma of her Beloved and best Friend.

Sometimes, God heals but life is still painful. If Alaine's healing were simply God giving her a happy life in exchange for tragedy, she wouldn't be in a motorized wheelchair and wouldn't still be suffering as she is. What God has done in Alaine's life is even more profound than removing her pain. He has turned her tragedy into triumph.

Because of how she suffered and still suffers, Alaine can speak a unique hope and comfort into the lives of others who also suffer. Whether ministering to "her girls" in a prison or communicating God's love to victims of sex trafficking, Alaine's history gives her the right to declare hope when there seems to be none.

Do you remember being a kid, standing in line for a thrilling roller coaster or a scary movie, trying to give yourself courage? One trick I (Juli) always played was to find someone who looked younger and smaller than I was. I'd say to myself, "If she can do this, then I can too." Courage is contagious!

This is certainly true when it comes to Alaine. Women across the world walking along the painful road of healing from sexual abuse have been given courage just by watching her. "When I look in Alaine's eyes, I see Jesus. If she can have so much joy and peace after what she's been through, maybe I can too. I have hope that someday I can be like Alaine."

Your Invitation to Victory

Dear friend, your healing journey is about more than managing your anguish and fear. The Healer has bigger plans for you than a pain-free life. He intends to transform your story into one of victory.

The women you have met in these pages have each experienced a different version of brokenness. They each met the Healer in a unique way and are at different stages of their healing journey. Yet each one declares, "God is my Healer. He is redeeming my pain!" All of them have watched God transform their tragedy into triumph. In her own way, each one is comforting others with the comfort that she has received.

We hope that each of their stories has encouraged and inspired you. But remember . . . this book is not about them. Yes, they are courageous, tenacious, and faithful, but their stories are written to exalt only ONE, Jehovah Rapha.

Hebrews chapter 11 is often referred to as the Hall of Fame of Faith. The author highlights many of the great men and woman who trusted God in dire circumstances. Over and over again, we read, "By faith . . ." (Enoch, Noah, Sarah, Abraham, Rahab, and so on). The chapter names real people who trusted God in spite of great hardship and trials. In some ways, the book you hold in your hands is a modern-day version of Hebrews 11. Each one of these nine women, by faith, ran to Jehovah Rapha with her grief, despair, doubts, and pain.

Hebrews 12 begins this way:

Therefore, since we are surrounded by such a great cloud of witnesses, let us throw off everything that hinders and the sin that so easily entangles. And let us run with perseverance the race marked out for us, fixing our eyes on Jesus, the pioneer and perfecter of faith.

Your new friends—Marian, Hope, Lorraine, Ann, Angel, Amy, Rita, Kathy, and Alaine—are your cloud of witnesses as you face the reality of your own brokenness. They told you their stories for one purpose: to proclaim that there is a Healer. His name is Jesus and He is worthy of your faith and worship! Will you fix your eyes upon Him?

Can you hear the chorus of these nine women singing with one voice:

> *Don't give up! Don't give up!*
> *Keep on keeping on.*
> *The Healer is at work!*
> *He is praying for you.*
> *We are praying for you.*
> *Hope and healing can be yours!*

NOTES

Chapter 1: Surprised by the Healer

1. We have written extensively about this in our Bible study *Passion Pursuit*. If you would like to find out more about how sexuality is a holy metaphor and why it is so sacred, we encourage you to go through this study.

2. R. Laird Harris, Gleason L. Archer Jr., and Bruce K. Waltke, eds., *Theological Wordbook of the Old Testament* (Chicago: Moody, 1999), 857.

Chapter 2: Marian's Story

1. Portions of this chapter are used by permission from the book by Marian Green *Inviting Intimacy: Overcoming the Lies of Shame,* releasing July, 2016 (Wesleyan Publishing House: wphstore.com).

Chapter 3: Hope's Story

1. Diana J. Dell, *Memorable Quotations: American Women Writers of the Past* (Lincoln, NE: Writers Club Press, 2000), 89.

Chapter 4: Lorraine's Story

1. R. T. Kendall, *How to Forgive Ourselves Totally* (Lake Mark, FL: Charisma House, 2007), 6.

2. William Arndt, Frederick W. Danker, and Walter Bauer, *A Greek-English Lexicon of the New Testament and Other Early Christian Literature* (Chicago: University of Chicago Press, 2000), 597.

3. See 2 Corinthians 2:11 NLT.

Chapter 5: Ann's Story

1. David G. Benner, *The Gift of Being Yourself* (Downers Grove, IL: IVP, 2004), 47.

2. Ibid., 48.

Chapter 6: Angel's Story

1. Eric Metaxas, *Miracles: What They Are, Why They Happen, and How They Can Change Your Life* (New York: Dutton, 2014), 17.

Chapter 7: Amy's Story

1. http://faith-forward.org/three-dollars--worth-of-god.htm.

2. Andrew Murray, *The Practice of God's Presence* (New Kensington, PA: Whitaker House, 2000), 221.

Chapter 8: Rita's Story

1. R. T. Kendall, *Total Forgiveness* (Lake Mary, FL: Charisma House, 2002), xxvii.

2. Phillip Yancey, "An Unnatural Act," *Christianity Today* (April 8, 1991): 39.

3. Martha Kilpatrick, *All and Only* (Suches, GA: Shulamite, 1998), 25–26.

Chapter 9: Kathy's Story

1. For more information on the treatment of vaginismus, see vaginismus.com.

2. Dr. Paul Brand and Philip Yancey, *Pain: The Gift Nobody Wants* (New York: HarperCollins, 1993), 12.

3. C. S. Lewis, *The Problem of Pain* (San Francisco: HarperOne, 2015), 3.

Chapter 10: Alaine's Story

1. Adapted from Alaine Pakkala, *The Roar of the Lamb: A True Story* (Colorado Springs: Lydia Discipleship, 2014), 9–10.

2. Ibid., 12–18.

3. Ibid., 40–45.

4. Adapted from Anonymous, *Laura: A True Story* (Deeper Walk International), 141–43.

5. Alaine Pakkala, *Taking Every Thought Captive* (Colorado Springs: Lydia Press, 1995), 3–4.

A Ten-Week Bible Study

Dear Friend,

We are excited about what God is going to do in your life as a result of your choice to do this study. It is good to read a book, but even better when you get into *the Book*, God's Word, for yourself. Psalm 119:11 (NASB) declares, "Your Word I have treasured in my heart, that I may not sin against You."

To help you treasure God's Word in your heart, we suggest you do three things each week:

1. Memorize a verse
2. Meditate on it
3. Pray the verse back to God

Why memorize God's Word? As a wise woman said, "When you memorize God's Word, you increase the Holy Spirit's vocabulary in your life."

Why meditate? As another wise woman said, "When you meditate on Scripture, it sinks down deep into your heart and becomes part of who you are."

Why pray? Prayer is a way of personalizing what God is teaching you.

At the end of each week's study, you'll be encouraged to write down your responses to the following questions—What did I learn this week about the Healer? What did I learn about myself?—and then to write a prayer to accept the Healer's invitation. If you feel you can't accept the invitation, express your feelings and fears honestly to your God. He is big enough to handle all our doubts, our whys, our everythings.

We believe you are holding this book in your hands because Jehovah Rapha, the Healer, longs to bring hope and healing to you, His precious daughter.

May you be surprised by how much He loves you!

We are praying for you!

Linda and Juli

P.S. Some of the questions in this study are personal. You can choose to share your answer or not share your answer with your group.

Week 1

Read chapter 1, "Surprised by the Healer," at least once. Twice would be better.

1. Memory verse: Psalm 139:1. Write it here.

   A *little lesson in memorizing and meditating*: Type the memory verse into your iPhone, iPad, or whatever gadget you use, or do it the old-fashioned way and write it on a 3x5 card and tape it to your bathroom mirror. Repeat the verse over and over until you can say it from memory, asking God to burn the words into your heart and mind, to make them part of you.

2. Read Psalm 139 and write a paragraph to describe how it makes you feel that God knows and cares about every part of you.

3. Read the women's questions on pages 11–12. What surprised you about the women's questions?

4. What two or three questions do you think women are asking today about sexuality?

5. Read Psalm 147:3. List three words that describe how this verse makes you feel.

6. Why do you think women are so hesitant to ask God to bring healing in their sexual brokenness?

7. Have you ever seen Jehovah Rapha heal a friend in her sexuality? What did it look like? Have you ever received sexual healing from Him? If so, what did it look like for you?

8. Describe why you think women believe the lie "You may be forgiven but you can never be whole." Do you believe it?

9. Read Isaiah 61:1–3. Write a paragraph describing the three exchanges that happen in verse 3? What does this mean to you personally?

10. What did you learn about the Healer this week?

11. What did you learn about yourself this week?

12. Write a prayer responding to the invitation in chapter 1. Or pray this prayer:
    God, I'm scared, but I want to know You as Jehovah Rapha. I open my heart, my mind to You to learn of You as Healer. I'm ready to be surprised!

Jehovah Rapha invites you to open yourself up to His healing. He is waiting to surprise you, so run to Him!

Week 2

Read chapter 2, "Marian's Story," and the invitation at least once. Twice would be better.

1. Memory verse: John 8:32. Write it here.

2 Did anything surprise you about Marian's story?

3. Marian asked the Lord to be her Healer. Do you think women long for God to be their Healer but fail to ask Him to heal them? Where are you in your healing journey?

4. God asked Marian to identify the lies she had believed. She had to look back, even though it was difficult. Has God asked you to look back? The lies you believe may be different from Marian's. Ask the Healer to expose those lies and then write them here.

5. Marian's journey was about unearthing the lies she believed and embracing God's truth. She asked to learn about sexual intimacy and God began to show her about spiritual intimacy.

Read Deuteronomy 6:5 and write your own definition of spiritual intimacy from this verse.

6. We see in Proverbs 5 that the battle between Satan's lies and God's truth has been going on forever. Read Proverbs 5 twice. Paraphrase verses 1–14, and then make a list of the main lessons the father is teaching his son. What lies does he instruct the son to stay away from?

7. In Proverbs 5:14–20 there is an abrupt change. Paraphrase these verses and then make a list of the primary lessons the father instructs the son to follow.

8. List at least three things you learn personally about God's view of sexual intimacy in Proverbs 5:15–19. How is God asking you to apply this truth if you are married? If you are single?

9. What did you learn about God this week?

10. What did you learn about yourself this week?

11. Write a prayer responding to God's invitation to you.

Week 3

Read chapter 3, "Hope's Story," and the invitation at least once. Twice would be better.

1. Memory verse: Psalm 32:5. Write it here.

2. What surprised you about Hope's story?

3. Read Psalm 32 out loud. Write a paragraph describing what David learned about his sin and forgiveness in verses 1–5.

4. How can you relate to what David experienced?

5. Read Psalm 32:6–7. David found a new hiding place, not a place of shame and sin. How do you think he found this wonderful hiding place?

6. Read Psalm 32:8–10. The speaker seems to change from David in verses 6–7 to God in verses 8–10. What does God promise?

7. List at least three things that David gained by confessing his sin and coming out of hiding.

8. List at least three things that Hope gained by confessing her sin and coming out of hiding.

9. What did you learn about God this week?

10. What did you learn about yourself this week?

11. How can you make Psalm 32 real in your life? What does it look like for you to come out of hiding?

For Reflection

The enemy knows that healing doesn't come when we hide in darkness but instead when we step into the light. He desperately wants us to be bound by secrets. When Hope was silent, the enemy was winning. Hope determined, "I have to quit hiding from myself . . . from God. Right here. Right now."

Week 4

Read chapter 4, "Lorraine's Story," and the invitation at least once. Twice would be better.

1. Memory verse: Psalm 51:1. Write it here.

2. In Psalm 51, David describes the blessing of forgiveness, which follows conviction and confession. David wrote Psalm 51 after his sin with Bathsheba. Read Psalm 51 out loud. What does this psalm teach you about David?

3. If you had a friend who was in agony as Lorraine was, what would you say to help her understand what it means to forgive yourself? Write your answer here, using what you have learned from Lorraine's story.

4. Read Revelation 12:10. Who is the accuser and where does he accuse?

5. Because Satan's job description is to make you feel guilty, you need to learn to fight against his accusations. First, recognize the voice. Explain how you do that.

Second, remember the cross. How did Lorraine do this? How will you do this?

Third, declare the truth! Read James 4:7 and 1 Peter 5:8—9. Write a paraphrase of these verses here and pray your paraphrase out loud, telling God that you are choosing to resist the enemy and stand in God's truth.

6. Lorraine *knew* the truth about forgiveness but struggled to make it practical in her life. Here are some practical things you can do to break free from the enemy's accusations:

On a piece of paper, write a list of your sins.

- Get alone with your God for fifteen to thirty minutes—on a walk or on your knees . . . wherever it can be just you and your Father.
- Read your list out loud, confessing your sin to your God who loves you.
- Love keeps no record of wrongs. So, tear up your list or burn it! Destroy it! Your wrongs are forgiven.

7. What did you learn about God this week?

8. What did you learn about yourself this week?

9. Write a prayer thanking God that you can walk in forgiveness.

Week 5

Read chapter 5, "Ann's Story," and the invitation at least once. Twice would be better.

1. Memory verse: Psalm 139:14. Write it here.

2. Read 2 Kings 5:1–14. Why do you think Naaman was furious?

3. Do you think that people today believe that God should heal their wounds in a certain way? Have you ever become angry when He didn't heal your wounds the way you thought He would? Explain why.

4. Read Mark 1:40–45. How did this amazing healing differ from Naaman's healing?

5. Which healing would you want and why—Naaman's or the leper's?

6. God is a wonderful Healer. He can heal instantly or by asking us to dunk ourselves in a river seven times. If Ann had been asked how she wanted God to heal her, we think she would have said, "Heal me quickly; heal me with one word!" But God's way was "many trips to the river" over many years.

   Reread the verses on page 80 that revealed truth in how God sees Ann's body and how He sees yours. Write here the two verses that speak to your heart and share why they speak to you.

7. Write a paragraph describing how the section called "Burying Barbie" affected you.

8. Did you know God can redeem your scars? Ann wrote: "Scars remind us where we have been, but they do not have to dictate where we are going." What physical, emotional, sexual scars do you have?

9. Write a prayer asking God to redeem your scars so they do not dictate where you are going.

10. What role do you think God is asking you to have in your healing journey?

11. You are invited to take a step! Reread Ann's Statement of Truth on pages 87–88. Spend some time alone with God, asking Him to give you your own Statement of Truth. Write it here.

Week 6

Read chapter 6, "Angel's Story," and the invitation at least once. Twice would be better.

1. Memory verse: 1 John 4:10—11. These two verses are Angel's story. God loves Angel with His radical love and now she loves others as God loved her. Write the verses here.

2. Write what surprised you about Angel's story?

3. Have you ever prayed, *God, I want to encounter Your radical love for me?* Why do you think women would be afraid to pray this?

4. Read Psalm 103 out loud. Make a list of all you learn about God's amazing love for you in verses 8—18.

5. Using Psalm 103 (and your list), praise and thank the Lord for who He is and how He loves you.

6. God used Becky to be His arms of love to Angel. Think about someone God has used to reveal His love to you. Write about this person here.

7. List three things that keep you from praying, *God, let Your radical love pour through me to others.*

8. Are you willing to pray this prayer and be God's arms of love to someone? Why or why not?

9. What did you learn about God this week?

10. What did you learn about yourself this week?

11. Write a prayer responding to the invitation to encounter Jesus' radical love.

Week 7

Read chapter 7, "Amy's Story," and the invitation at least once. Twice would be better.

1. Memory verse: Hebrews 4:12. Write it here.

    Ask God to show you this week how His Word is alive, powerful, sharper, cutting, and exposing. Come ready to share at Bible study what the Lord reveals to you.

2. What surprised you about Amy and Tim's story?

3. Reread the four things God asked Amy to do on her journey to rebuild trust (pages 110–12). Which one do you identify with? Explain why.

4. Read Matthew 18:21–35 and describe what you learn about forgiveness.

5. Amy and Tim encountered Jesus as their personal Savior and God's *dunamis* power became evident in their lives. Where are you in your personal journey of experiencing *dunamis* power? Write about it here.

6. Read Romans 5:3–5. As you do, imagine that a friend of yours has a problem in her marriage. Then write an email to her using these verses as an encouragement of what God can do in the midst of her pain.

7. How have you seen God work the truth of Romans 5:3–5 in your life?

8. Why do you think a wife's favorite three-word prayer is *Change HIM, Lord*?

9. What is your favorite three-word prayer?

10. Read Psalm 139:23–24 out loud, asking God to search your heart. Be still before Him and write down anything He reveals to you.

11. What did you learn about God this week?

12. What did you learn about yourself this week?

13. Write a prayer responding to God's invitation to encounter His *dunamis* power.

Week 8

Read chapter 8, "Rita's Story," and the invitation at least once. Twice would be better.

1. Memory verses: Matthew 6:12, 14. Write the verses here.

2. What surprised you about Rita's story?

3. What did you think about Rita's unspoken arrangement with God?

4. Have you ever had an unspoken arrangement with God? Explain.

5. Read Ephesians 4:30–32. Write a paraphrase of these verses here.

6. How do you feel knowing your bitter spirit grieves the Holy Spirit? How does knowing this motivate you to make the choice to forgive?

7. List three things you learned about forgiveness this week from Rita's story.

8. Rita said, "I don't think any of us know what we really believe until what we want is taken away, damaged, or threatened." Explain why you agree or disagree.

9. Reread about Joseph's broken dreams on page 136. Write a paragraph describing how you hope to move past asking, "God, why?" to asking, "How can I please God?" and "What is Your will here?" (To read the whole story of Joseph, go to Genesis chapters 37, 39–50.)

10. What did you learn about God this week?

11. What did you learn about yourself this week?

12. If you are willing to accept the invitation to make peace with a broken life, consider praying David's prayer from Psalm 31:14–15 (NASB):

> *But as for me, I trust in You, O Lord,*
> *I say, "You are my God."*
> *My times are in Your hand.*

Week 9

Read chapter 9, "Kathy's Story," and the invitation at least once. Twice would be better.

1. Memory verse: James 1:2. Write it here.

2. What surprised you most about Kathy's story?

3. Have you ever considered a time of pain and trial as "joy," or "a gift," or "a friend"? Explain why or why not.

4. Read James 1:2–4 and Romans 5:3–5. List all you receive when you accept pain and trials with joy.

5. Which of these things do you need most?

6. Read 2 Corinthians 1:3–4. Imagine that you have a friend who is in deep pain. Write her a note of encouragement here, using what you learned from James 1:2–4; Romans 5:3–5; and 2 Corinthians 1:3–4.

7. Describe a time God comforted you in your pain.

8. How has God used you to comfort others with the comfort He has given you?

9. Read 1 Peter 5:7 in several different versions (your favorite version, Phillips, Amplified, The Message, and so on). Write out the version that touches you the most.

10. Make a list of all you have learned about God this week.

11. Make a list of all you have learned about yourself this week.

Dear Friend, your great God who loves you is inviting you to cast your pain on Him. Spend fifteen to thirty minutes in the outdoors talking to God about your pain. Thank Him that He cares for you affectionately and watchfully. Thank Him that HE carries your pain for you! Ask Him to give you the strength to see the gift in your pain.

Week 10

Read chapter 10, "Alaine's Story," and the invitation at least once. Twice would be better.

1. Memory verse: Romans 12:2. Write it here.

2. What inspired you about Alaine's story?

3. Write a paragraph describing what you learned from Alaine about being transformed by the renewing of your mind.

4. Read Psalm 119:11. We are not going to memorize all the Psalms and the entire New Testament—and you probably aren't either—but what steps can you take to treasure God's Word in your heart? Ask God for personal steps for you and write at least three here.

5. Read the two paragraphs from Alaine's Bible study on pages 167–68. How would you explain these truths about the spiritual battle to a friend? Write your thoughts here.

6. What trial or tragedy in your life do you want God to turn into triumph? Read 2 Corinthians 2:14. Write a prayer to God, asking Him to make this true in your life.

7. In this book you have met nine courageous women— Marian, Hope, Lorraine, Ann, Angel, Amy, Rita, Kathy, and Alaine—who have honestly and intimately shared their sorrows and their joys with you. We're sure that you learned something from each of them. Look back through their stories. Which woman did you most identify with? Write down why here.

8. How have you been surprised by the Healer during this study?

9. How have you grown in your faith journey with the Lord Jesus in this study?

We pray that this book and Bible study is only the beginning of your healing journey. We join with your new friends, Marian, Hope, Lorraine, Ann, Angel, Amy, Rita, Kathy, and Alaine, as a chorus with one voice singing:

> Don't give up
> Please don't give up
> Keep on keeping on
> The Healer is at work
> He is praying for you
> We are praying for you
> Hope and healing are for you!

Acknowledgments

The invisible woman behind this project is Liz Heaney. Thank you, Liz, amazing editor, for your prayer, direction, and encouragement!

Thanks to our friend and encourager Judy Dunagan and the rest of the Moody Publishers team for their excitement and encouragement about this project. We appreciate you.

We thank Ginger Taddeo and her Bible study group in Akron, Ohio, for being the pilot study of *Surprised by the Healer*.

We thank our wonderful Authentic Intimacy team who has cheered us on each step of the way. Thank you for the protection and the strength the Lord provided through your prayers.

We are blessed among women to have Jody and Mike as husbands. Thank you for holding us up in prayer and encouraging us each step of the way. We couldn't have written this book without you!

Pursuing passion takes time, intentionality, and creativity.

ALSO
AVAILABLE IN
SPANISH

DVD CONTAINS
ENGLISH AND SPANISH
TRANSLATIONS

Passion Pursuit offers a valuable and sacred journey to joy and freedom. This daring ten-week study combines the psychological expertise of Dr. Juli Slattery, formerly of Focus on the Family, along with bestselling author and beloved Bible teacher Linda Dillow. They are from two different generations but share a passion to bring God's truth and healing to women in their marriages and their lives.

MOODY
Publishers™

From the Word to Life